THE RINGSIDE BOOK OF

BOXING

THE RINGSIDE BOOK OF
BOXING

O. F. SNELLING

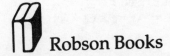

Robson Books

First published in Great Britain in hardback by Pelham Books Ltd
under the title *A Bedside Book of Boxing,* 1972
This paperback edition published in 1991 by Robson Books Ltd,
Bolsover House, 5 – 6 Clipstone Street, London W1P 7EB

British Library Cataloguing in Publication Data
Snelling, O. F.
  The ringside book of boxing
  I. Title II. [A bedside book of boxing]
  796.83

ISBN 0 86051 767 5

Printed in Great Britain by
Billing & Sons Ltd, Worcester, Worcs.

To
the memory of
A. J. LIEBLING

Contents

Acknowledgements

The author would like to thank the publishers for permission to quote from the following works.

The Sweet Science A. J. Liebling; Gollancz

Jack Johnson – In the Ring – And Out; National Sports Publishing Co.

A Man Must Fight Gene Tunney; Cape

The Web and the Rock Thomas Wolfe; Heinemann

Two Fisted Jeff Hugh Fullerton; Consolidated Book Publishers

Portrait of Hemingway Lillian Ross; Penguin

Round by Round Jack Dempsey; Chapman & Hall

Prides of the Fancy Trevor Wignall; Nash & Grayson

Introduction

Sport, as a term, covers a very wide field. To some people, now increasingly on the decrease, so to speak, it means bagging birds on and after the Glorious Twelfth. These gentry, if they are sufficiently able to sit astride a saddle, will also tally-ho with the best of them after the unfortunate fox. The unspeakable in full pursuit of the uneatable?

The gentleman who is reputed with having coined that particular phrase no doubt had a very different idea of sport. It is certain that he 'sported his oak' in his Oxford days, and no less certain that he visited 'sporting houses' during his London period. After all, he *was* ambisextrous. Yes, Oscar Wilde must definitely have viewed the term in a rather different sense than that of a particular acquaintance of his: the Marquess of Queensberry, who eventually caused his ruination.

I am inclined to take the word in its athletic sense, that is, as an indoor or outdoor physical endeavour in which both or all parties stand a chance – shall we say a *sporting* chance?

By this definition, I would include what are – to me – quite daft exploits, like climbing the Matterhorn, or the Eiffel Tower by its rivets! And even bull-fighting, in which, at least, there are willing participants on both sides, whatever else one's feelings might be about the matter.

At the other extreme, I would also include ostensibly mild and unfatiguing pastimes like croquet on the lawn, which, to my own knowledge, can engender more rage and bad feeling than any sport with which I am acquainted.

But I definitely exclude rape and white-slave trafficking. Black-slave trafficking, too, for that matter. I bracket all these with bird-shooting, fox-hunting, and pig-sticking – done just for the thrill of the chase.

Personally, as far as excitement and entertainment are concerned, I prefer baseball to cricket, the American style of football to ours – after some of the games I've seen recently – and heterosexuality to homosexuality. But I would accept them all as valid sports, provided the activity is *between consenting parties,* and no harm is done to anyone involved against his or her will.

Thus, I hate war, torture, and all forms of physical and mental violence perpetrated in the name of some ideal, simply because it is quite certain that one or both sides involved isn't relishing the business.

I also flinch from injury and mutilation committed in cold blood, however necessary it might be. I am quite certain that I would faint or vomit were I obliged to witness a surgical operation. I am just as sure that I would not be much help at a street accident involving a man, a woman, or a child. I have had qualms at the sight of a dog or a cat run down: what I would do at the sight of a human in a similar plight I cannot imagine. So far, I have been spared a gory accident.

Yet I have sat and watched boxing matches like the first Mills-Lesnevich encounter and the Baksi-Woodcock meeting, without turning a hair. In the one there was blood almost by the bucket-full and in the other what appeared to be, to the uninitiated, a horrible, one-sided slaughter.

This second fight was a pretty grim affair, I admit. But my whole argument is that nobody *forced* Bruce Woodcock into that Harringay ring at gun-point. Nobody inveigled him into an arduous profession for peanuts in order to get him bashed almost insensible. He did what he did primarily because he enjoyed doing it, and also because he thrived handsomely during the few years he was at the top. He went into the professional ring for the cash he could take out of it.

Incidentally, when Woodcock retired well after that Baksi fight, still in full possession of all his faculties, his earnings were said to be well over £100,000. In 1950, that was worth a hell of a lot more than it is now. Bruce had never been a wild spender, and most of that money was still intact and well-invested. Had he never taken up boxing for a living he would probably still be slogging away in the Doncaster railway yards.

Professional pugilism is a brutal business: I have no argument about that. But it is also a scientific one. Further, in my submission, it is a sport. A lot of other people will give you quite an argument about *that,* and some of them are the very same people who will defend that 'sport of kings', horse-racing, which, looking at some aspects, is one of the rottenest and crookedest forms of endeavour known to man or beast!

Boxing at its worst is vile. It can be dull and terribly boring to watch at times. It has been, and still is, a form of financial exploitation, in certain cases, although it need not be, with more rigorous control. Also, most of Baroness Summerskill's almost now-legendary censures are, in my opinion, perfectly valid.

Yes, too many punches around the cranium *will* eventually scramble your brains. But you only need to miss your footing just once on the side of the Eiger to scramble them much more quickly and far, far more effectively.

I have seen, by diagram and model, what happens to the human brain each time a fist thuds against a jaw or a temple, and I know perfectly well what can occur if the brain is subjected to too many of these punches, too often. But the Summerskills of this world and her present-day disciples underrate the practitioners of pugilism, and appear to imagine that professional boxers have never seen or heard of a punch-drunk fighter.

The fact is that fighters well know their occupational hazards. So, for that matter, do coal-miners. They know what silicosis can do to their lungs, and what the roof falling in can do to the rest of their bodies, just as operators of pneumatic drills are well aware at what can happen to *them* in the long run, with their brains and bodies being continually shaken forcibly for hour after hour each day.

Why don't baronesses ever campaign against mining and road excavation? And did it never occur to such 'do-gooders' that colliers and road-workers often took to fighting for a living as the *lesser* of two evils?

The obvious argument against all this, of course, is that coal and roads are absolute essentials to our society, and that in these enlightened days the people who produce them for us are very handsomely paid. This I gladly admit – although the bosses took a hell of a long time getting round to it! But it doesn't make the production of these boons any the less unpleasant for the producers of coal and roads. I'd rather take my chances with Mike Tyson in the ring than spend a day hewing coal down a particularly dodgy pit.

Boxing at its best is magnificent. It can be artistic, dramatic, and extremely exciting. At times it is positively heroic! It has often been highly remunerative for its better exponents: making millions for the men who might have considered themselves fortunate to possess ten or twenty quid at one time during their whole lives had they never entered the ring.

That about 75 per cent of these same men lived very well and spent prodigally while they had the stuff and later reverted to the penury they had known earlier after it had all gone, as in the case of people like Beau Jack, may be the basis of a powerful argument against a social system and proper education, but not, I submit, against the trade of professional boxing in itself.

I have suggested that boxing is an art, although only rarely can it honestly be termed a noble one. It does *not*, as has often been claimed, help to build the characters of individuals. At least, I have met with hardly any examples of its doing so. In my experience, which is a very wide and long one, boxers are neither more nor less noble than anyone else. They are just very nice people, on the whole, although you occasionally do get a few rotten apples.

This is despite the once-held belief that the practice of boxing was supposed to be one of the factors that had raised the honourable and upright Briton above the conglomerous mass of wops, nignogs, and dagoes – the ring used to be considered a sort of plebian equivalent of the playing-fields of Eton. If all this were true, those very same wops, nignogs, and dagoes should now be just as noble and upright as we are: the wonderful Brits – and that's a very disturbing thought to some people, living left-overs of the old Raj – for there is no denying that they wield their fists a damned sight better than we do nowadays!

The foregoing is, in part, my justification for endorsing an activity which has had more than its fair share of knocks and criticisms – particularly since Steve Watt died from the results of a hard fight.

Other people defend and justify boxing in rather different ways. Some go as far as to state, quite openly and often quite honestly, their belief that there is nothing rotten, crooked, dangerous, or ignoble about boxing at all.

One or two people, not quite so naive, put up a pretty good case. One, the late A.J. Liebling, who happens to be among my favourite writers, once stated what I think is a very amusing defence on behalf of his particular sport. His risibility should not detract from his argument. I think he is well worth quoting:

A fighter's hostilities are not turned inward, like a Sunday tennis player's, or a lady MP's. They come out naturally with his sweat, and when his job is done he feels good because he has

16

expressed himself. Chain-of-command types, to whom this is intolerable, try to rationalise their envy by proclaiming solicitude for the fighter's health. If a boxer, for example, ever went as crazy as Nijinsky, all the wowsers in the world would be screaming 'Punch-drunk'. Well, who hit Nijinsky? And why isn't there a campaign against ballet? It gives girls thick legs. If a novelist who lived exclusively on applecores won the Nobel Prize, vegetarians would chorus that the repulsive nutriment had invigorated his brain. But when the prize goes to Ernest Hemingway, who has been a not particularly evasive boxer for years, no one rises to point out that the percussion has apparently stimulated his intellection. Albert Camus, the French probable for the Nobel, is an ex-boxer, too.

Another writer, someone rather less than my favourite one, held a very different view. J.L. Manning, who used to be on the *Daily Mail*, didn't like boxing, and he consistently waged war against it for many years. He claimed that it was both brutal *and* degrading, and he let pass no opportunity to give it a dig. He was just as much entitled to his opinion, of course, as anyone else is to the opposite one, but his words would have rung a little truer to me had he not forever been taking up the cudgels on behalf of some minority or lost cause in the various sports – and, incidentally, on behalf of the sales of the particular paper he happened to be working for.

I have no quarrel with J.L. Manning when he cited examples of fights that were 'pitiful to watch', or which affected him so much 'that I was nearly sick at the ringside'. Nor do I take issue with him when he made the most of those two Clay-Liston affairs. I am inclined to agree with him whole-heartedly here as far as the degradation side is concerned, although surely there was the very minimum of brutality in both of those contests – all seven rounds lumped together? The only brutality I can remember was that waged against those cash customers in the United States and the poor television viewers over here in Britain who stayed up until past three in the morning and held their eyes open to watch a one-round fiasco via the satellite.

What annoys me about J.L. Manning, particularly, is that he should have cocked his leg across his hobby-horse with a full column 'Last Word' in a sort of obituary-cum-homily after the report that Freddie Mills had shot himself.

If Mills had become a hoodlum, back in the 1930s, instead of a booth-fighter, and had forged his way to material prosperity by the use of the knuckle-duster and the strong-arm stuff at the expense of harmless 'little' people who hadn't the means to fight back, he could have made his pile in relative anonymity. Later, he could have turned respectable in middle age, as many hoodlums have done, with a restaurant or a night-club to sustain him. Then, if financial difficulties had led him to take his own life, few people would have – or *could* have, for that matter – pointed to an early life of violence as the reason for suicide.

Similarly, if someone back in pre-war Bournemouth had noticed this Mills youth's ideal rugged physiognomy, high spirits, and natural flair for histrionics, and had encouraged *these,* rather than his genial pugnacity, we might have had a sort of English James Cagney or Jack Palance. A waning popularity or a shrinking bank balance, culminating in suicide, would never, surely, have then brought upon the entertainment business a diatribe like that of J.L. Manning's?

Freddie Mills forged for himself a household name, universal popularity, and considerable prosperity by bludgeoning his way to them in an admittedly hard profession for which he was ideally suited, and which he loved. If he was an insensitive thug who liked hurting just for hurting's sake, who carried on socking people after he had retired from the ring, I certainly never heard or read of it. Even Manning, who was fond of him, said 'he was too kind-hearted and too playful to be as mean as the reality of the ring must have its champions'.

And yet this journalist, on his hobby-horse, writing of the premature and sudden death of a business-man, who had apparently fallen upon hard times, must still see his demise 'as a tragedy which had its beginnings nearly twenty years ago and weaved the complex pattern of one man's life from its first violence to its last'.

It may be that I am blind, but for the life of me I can't see that.

Mountaineers, bobsleigh riders, and racing drivers face a far more hazardous life than any boxer. I would go so far as to say that the odds against their finishing up dead or with permanent injury are much shorter. The one great difference is that whereas rock-climbers and other death-dicers are doing their best to avoid injury, and that when it happens it is called an 'accident', the pugilist, in many people's eyes, deliberately attempts to inflict damage on his opponent while trying to elude it himself.

Isn't it about time that certain medical bodies started issuing reports on the amount of damage inflicted by the internal combustion-engine, on the racing track as well as on the roads? And isn't it about time that certain busybodies began handing out tracts to the exponents of dangerous sports other than those of boxing?

This book is a collection of more or less unrelated pieces about a sport which has fascinated me all my life. It has no chronological pattern, and no one section is, I hope, excessively long. On occasion, I allow myself considerable digression, because I believe that the subject I happen to be dealing with at the moment is worth digressing about, and holds interest. It is the sort of book I hope you can take to bed with you and dip into wherever you may chance to open it. Indeed, when it was first published some twenty years ago, I originally entitled it *A Bedside Book of Boxing*. It has now been out of print for many years, but I am glad to see it available once again, to be enjoyed – I also hope – by those of a younger generation who are breaking fresh ground in reading about these pugilistic heroes of the past. Very few of the characters I write about have not been written about many times before. The difference is, I think, that I approach them and write of them in a way that is at least fresh and unusual.

1   There Ain't No Justice

I like heavyweights. I like them very much, and I would always elect to witness a contest between two big fellows rather than one with a couple of tiny men performing. But I am under no illusions : skill and artistry are to be found, generally speaking, among those practitioners in the lighter divisions. The big money and the lion's share of publicity, of course, is reserved for the heavier men. I state the obvious when I say that the prospect of drama, uncertainty, and blood and snot flying about increase proportionately the larger the participants involved. This, and my predilection for heavyweights may be found to be a recurring theme in these pages.

One August evening in the Sixties, British television viewers were treated to a gala performance transmitted from San Remo by the Italian Television Service. It featured a bout between London's Golden Boy, Billy Walker, and an unranked Argentinian-cum-Italian named Eduardo Corletti, of whom few of us had ever heard. I think it is true to say that Walker's reputation as a big hitter had brain-washed the public into believing that we should see the sparks fly, with Corletti on his back after a round or two.

What actually happened was that Corletti, an elusive and light-hitting boxer, operated almost entirely on the retreat, counter-punching very effectively for the whole ten rounds. He didn't accomplish anything very spectacular himself, but he did make Walker look even less spectacular. Billy went forward from start to finish, but he also walked into innumerable jabs and hooks, and he made more swiping misses and bumble-footed stumbles than I have ever seen him make in any other contest. The decision of the three ringside judges of a draw, in my opinion, robbed Corletti, who boxed the affair in the only way his talents and limitations allowed. It also flattered Billy Walker. Although he went on to bash his way through a number of other highly-publicised bouts, I think that this Corletti contest proved to the discerning observer that the Golden Boy would never make a champion. Be that as it may, he made a very large fortune.

By comparison, on the evening following that San Remo fight, an international bantamweight contest took place at Paisley, in Scotland. Walter McGowan boxed an American Negro named Ron Jones. This bout earned exactly six lines of reportage at the very bottom of the last column on the sports page of a national newspaper the following morning. Coincidentally, it was also the back page. Thus, McGowan's effort was dealt with briefly at the bottom, right-hand corner of the very last page. It was very lucky to be there at all. Had anything more momentous happened the previous day in the sporting world it might have got shoved right off the paper.

I confess that I missed it entirely at the time. In fact, I would have known nothing at all about it had not B.B.C.'s *Grandstand* elected to televise its highlights the following afternoon. It was magnificent. I rate it as possibly the best of all little Walter McGowan's performances. I also gained more aesthetic pleasure from watching it than I have enjoyed in all but perhaps half-a-dozen of the many hundreds of fights I have seen.

Billy Walker, the wild-fisted basher, will be remembered and talked about for years to come, in British pugilistic circles. Good luck to him : these are my sentiments, and I extend them sincerely. Unfortunately, it also happens to be bad luck to Walter McGowan – and I stress that these are *not my* sentiments – for the simple reason that nature endowed this magnificent little athlete with a frame which would have been more suited to a materially-successful jockey.

I know it's an overworked complaint in the vicinity of the ring, but truly, there *ain't* no justice.

2   Referees and Judges

In Great Britain all professional boxing contests are in the sole charge of one man : the referee. Not only does he control the boxers by issuing commands to break, to stop holding, and to retire out of distance when there is a knock-down, etc., but he also tots up the points on his score-card between rounds, and at the end of a bout almost immediately walks across to one or the other of the contestants and raises his arm as the winner.

Great Britain is one of the few areas in the world where this system of deciding a winner still prevails. In most others two judges, sitting outside the ring, also have a say in the matter. Thus, in the case of an extremely close match, one judge might vote boxer A as the winner, the other judge might vote boxer B as having won, and the referee's opinion decides which fighter gets the verdict.

Now, it has not been entirely unknown, on such occasions, for a howl to go up from the audience, followed by a chorus of boos. But cases of a subsequent wrecking of the joint, followed by a mass lynching of the officials, are negligible. Further, since two out of three of them voted for the same man as the winner, an irate partisan crowd is less inclined to think in terms of having witnessed daylight – or rather artificial light – robbery.

I can think of dozens of cases where I have watched bouts in this country, extremely closely-contested, with the referee, the sole adjudicator, giving the decision to the man *I* thought was the loser. A quite different referee might easily have seen things the opposite way. In certain cases, perhaps where a championship is involved, reputations can be won or lost in such a manner. The subsequent careers of one or both boxers can be affected enormously.

A particular example which comes to mind occurred in 1937. Today that fight is almost forgotten. It is better so, I suppose, because it was certainly a stinker. Ben Foord, the current British heavyweight champion, was defending his title against a capable but somewhat colourless challenger named Tommy Farr. After fifteen dull and desultory rounds, which, from my admittedly distant vantage-point, were mostly in favour of Foord, the referee walked to Farr's corner and raised his arm as the new British champion. The foghorn of boos which greeted Jack Hart's decision, from a non-partisan London element, which didn't care much either way, was immediately drowned by the inevitable 'Land of My Fathers', from an extremely partisan Welsh contingent, which cared very much.

The only really important thing about this particular fight

was that the winner had been scheduled to meet a visiting American by the name of Max Baer: a flamboyant personality whose antics and power of punch could be guaranteed to pack any hall in the country and to make front-page headline news in the papers.

Tommy Farr was the one who got this lucrative opportunity. He took full advantage of it by sticking his left fist into Max Baer's face persistently in an affair which was, if anything, less exciting than Foord's meeting with him a few weeks earlier. But whereas there had been some popular doubt as to whether Farr had bested Foord, there was none at all as to whether he had outpointed the great Max Baer. Overnight, Tommy Farr not only became a national hero, he was now a 'probable' in the world's championship stakes.

A month or two later, Farr sailed for New York City and boxed himself to temporary affluence but permanent fame in a very close world's title fight with the fabulous Joe Louis. (Incidentally, one judge made it very close, and the other judge and the referee were well in favour of Louis. Suppose that odd judge had been *refereeing* the fight under British conditions!)

Perhaps not entirely forgotten, but certainly overshadowed by the rise of Tommy Farr during the spring and summer of 1937, is the Max Baer-Ben Foord 'consolation' meeting in May of that year. It gives some idea of what might have been, had Foord retained his title in that waltz with Farr back in March. Baer knocked out Foord in nine thrilling rounds, each one of which was more exciting to the customers than any twelve or fifteen that Farr waged at this period.

As a much more recent example, there is the brave challenge of Howard Winstone for the featherweight championship of the world versus Vicente Saldivar, of Mexico, in 1965. I listened to the blow-by-blow commentary of this contest, on B.B.C. sound radio, like many thousands of others. The inter-round summaries were inevitably delivered by that experienced connoisseur of pugilism, W. Barrington Dalby. Throughout, he gave us the impression that Winstone was doing extremely well, and that he was slightly on top. In fact, although the Welsh challenger had a very bad fourteenth round, and we listeners had our hearts in our mouths for about three minutes, we were led to believe that if only Winstone could hold his own in the fifteenth and last round then the championship was his.

The referee, Bill Williams, thought differently. He had no hesitation at all in walking across to Saldivar and raising his arm at the conclusion of the bout. The papers, the following day, were pretty much in agreement that the decision was a just one, and the millions who watched a recording of the fight on television that same evening largely felt the same way.

Now I know for certain that a great many people have castigated W. Barrington Dalby, both in public and in private, for raising their hopes of a British victory. Some have cast doubts upon his credentials, and have even gone so far as to say that he was hopelessly incompetent at the particular job he had been doing for so many years.

The facts are – and I believe that only a small proportion of radio listeners were aware of it – that W. Barrington Dalby was one of the British Boxing Board of Control's foremost referees long before he ever became famous – or infamous, depending on your point of view – as an inter-round summarist. Two of the contests I recall his refereeing, and refereeing damned well, were the Benny Lynch-Peter Kane and Eric Boon-Arthur Danahar fights.

If he thought Winstone outpointed Saldivar, as he obviously did – and he could only have got closer to the two men than he was by standing up and taking a pace or two forward – then he 'called it as he saw it', as they say across the water. Further, had not W. Barrington Dalby been a *retired* boxing referee but an active one, there is more than an outside chance that it would have been he, and not Bill Williams, as the third man in the ring with Saldivar and Winstone. It follows, I think, that under such circumstances, Dalby would have proclaimed Howard Winstone the new featherweight champion of the world.

It is my opinion, as well as that of many other people, that the sooner Britain goes over to the two-judge system the better. A referee has enough to do controlling the boxers without having to bear the full responsibility of deciding which of them has accumulated the major share of points.

On rare occasions, after the referee has apportioned the points on his card between rounds, he tots them all up after the final bell and finds the score to be even. He then declares a draw. Now, a drawn verdict is a very unsatisfactory one, although you will often hear members of a boxing crowd say 'Fairest decision possible' when both fighters have waged a spirited and close contest which has been thoroughly appreciated. But this is sentiment speaking, rather than anything else.

It is very unlikely, despite the referee's tally, that the match was *absolutely* equal, and that the men concerned just couldn't be separated. It is as unlikely as the perfect dead heat in racing. I have, on many occasions, stood in the stands on the finishing line at places like Harringay, Walthamstow and the White City and watched two dogs streak by apparently neck-and-neck, or more appropriately, nose and nose. They have been so close that I have not dared to accept the odds offered by the bookies regarding which dog actually won. As far as I was concerned the race I had just watched *was* a dead heat. Invariably, after the prints of the photo-finish have been published, there is no doubt at all about the winner. Sometimes he wins by a nose : sometimes by as much as half a head. There is seldom any final argument about it. On such occasions I have been known to mutter something about a dead heat being the fairest result. This, of course, has been when my money was on the animal that was placed second or not placed at all.

Two judges, plus the referee, in boxing, should effectively take the place of the photo-finish camera. In some countries they have three judges. In the rare event of the officials' tallies coming even, either on the rounds won or points accumulated system, I think we might say that the fighters boxed a very, very close contest indeed. Only then could we honestly state that a draw is the fairest decision.

3 Ropes

The first time I ever saw photographs of boxing matches held in France, back in the early Thirties, I noticed that on each side of the ring the three horizontal ropes also had a vertical cord, or string, tying them together. The reason for this was immediately obvious. The natural elasticity of the ropes was not seriously impeded, but at the same time the vertical cord kept them more or less parallel when a boxer backed into them. It also lessened the chances of a fighter falling through the ropes and sustaining an injury.

At the time I wondered why other countries did not adopt this idea. It was certainly not employed in Great Britain or the United States.

Then, in 1938, at Harringay Arena, Eddie Phillips boxed Jack Doyle. The encounter was brief. Phillips was immeasurably the better boxer, and at times he made Doyle look crude, but Doyle was a fearful puncher, and he was always dangerous. They waged an exciting first round, which saw Phillips almost straight-lefting Doyle to death, but with the big Irishman staggering his man every time he got through with a right-hander, and dropping him to his knees on more than one occasion. Round two was short, dramatic, but very disappointing. Doyle forced Phillips to the ropes, sent him a telegram, as they say, of what he was about to do, and hurled over that terrible right fist. Eddie Phillips had not the slightest difficulty in side-stepping. Jack Doyle's punch struck nothing at all solid, and the impetus of his blow carried him head-first through the ropes, right over the ringside pressmen, and into the front aisle on to his Irish noggin.

Now you can see this sort of performance quite regularly by wrestlers. If it doesn't happen at least once in every tournament you can count yourself cheated, and you should demand your money back. But wrestlers, besides being just wrestlers, are also proficient acrobats and high divers. Jack Doyle, who later became a wrestler himself, and grew quite adept as a tumbler, was not quite so agile at this time. He knocked himself out at Harringay in 1938 when he landed on that floor. I would count this occasion as the high spot among the several expensive fiascos featuring the quite unpredictable Jack Doyle.

I have noticed that ever since then, almost every boxing tournament in Britain has been graced by that continental vertical cord holding the three horizontal ropes in check. It does not yet appear to be an integral part of the anatomy of the ring in the United States. It *was* used in, I think, the third meeting between Patterson and Johansson, but I can recall no other important occasion.

Strangely enough, it does not seem to be utilised in wrestling! Why? Because its object is to *prevent* participants from shooting headlong out of the ring. Anyone still in doubt as to whether such meetings are *bona fide* contests or inspired theatrical exhibitions should do some profound pondering upon this point.

4 Did Jack Johnson Quit?

Both the long search for a White Hope and the coloured Jack Johnson's extended and infamous reign as champion of the world came to an end on the afternoon of Monday, 5 April, 1915, in a sunlit ring erected on the race-course at Oriental Park, Havana, Cuba. This fight set up a new record for length in a heavyweight title contest under Marquess of Queensberry rules: a record which still stands, and which will now probably stand for ever. It lasted twenty-six rounds and ended when a superbly-fit and younger man floored the ageing, half-trained Negro for the full count.

It would, of course, be a fitting climax to this era of the mighty black champion if one were able to write of his defeat in much the same way as the defeats of some of his predecessors. Time and again champions have ended their reigns in a blaze of glory, going down in a manner which has stirred the emotions of sporting enthusiasts the whole world over. For something like eight years Jack Johnson had ruled the roost, and for the better part of that time millions of men and women had been looking forward to the day when a man could be found to beat him. Many times opinions had been voiced regarding the manner in which he would be vanquished.

Some said that a white-skinned boxer would emerge who would be the Negro's peer in every department of the game : Jack Johnson would be beaten on his merits. Others believed Johnson to be a pugilist so far removed from the normal run of boxers that only death, retirement or middle age could be instrumental in his overthrow. But nearly all agreed that if he lost his title in the ring then whoever might succeed him would have to be an unusual man, and that the fight which marked the end of Johnson's tenure would be one worth going many miles to see.

Yet the fact is that the contest between Jack Johnson and Jess Willard caused very little excitement outside Cuba and some parts of the United States at the time, largely owing to the all-absorbing interest of the war that raged in Europe. And although the fight was lengthy and not without thrills in some of its stages, it was for the most part a dull and wearisome test of endurance. The challenger lacked most of the requirements that go to make a colourful title-holder and he won the battle because he was big and strong rather than by virtue of possessing exceptional fistic talents. Moreover, Jack Johnson prevented the advocates of white supremacy from crowing too much by signing a sworn affidavit to the effect that he was not beaten in fair fight but lay down and faked the knock-out in return for a financial consideration and a promise of leniency when he returned to the United States to face a prison sentence.

It should be mentioned here that the Negro had been a voluntary exile from his native land for several years. A federal charge that he had violated the Mann Act in transporting a woman from one state to another for an immoral purpose was based on events which had taken place back in 1909. Johnson fled the country after he was sentenced to serve one year and a day in the penitentiary and was fined $1,000, several years later. He claimed that 'it was a rank frame-up'. He justified his flight to Europe on the grounds that the charges were based on a law that was not in effect at the time he and the woman had been together, and legally was not operative against him.

29

There may be some truth in that. However, the authorities were well aware that this had been only one of a series of similar liaisons, many of which had occurred *after* the Mann Act was operative, but with the ladies in question not being quite so co-operative witnesses as Belle Schreiber, the girl of the 1909 jaunt. I am not attempting to justify Jack Johnson's attitude or the federal authorities' interpretation of the law : I merely state the facts. The Negro jumped a boat for France and faced a prison sentence in Leavenworth if ever he went back to the States.

Jack Johnson had had a very pleasant time in Europe during the period of his exile. Crowds flocked to see him in his numerous theatrical engagements, and if his serious appearances in the ring bordered on the farcical (one was versus a wrestler, and in another he claimed he broke an arm, yet got a draw!) at least the public paid to see him, which was the primary object of the exercise. But when war broke out in 1914 things became very different. Johnson discovered that now all efforts were being directed towards the successful prosecution of the war and that he was no longer the attraction or important personage he had been. He closed down his household in Paris and shifted to London, where some sort of social life was still going on. He was able to maintain himself and his entourage by sporadic stage work, but money was not rolling in at all easily. It is difficult to imagine what course the history of heavyweight boxing might have taken had not an American promoter arrived in England with a contract for Jack Johnson to defend his title again.

The promoter was Jack Curley, the suggested opponent was Jess Willard, and the site of the proposed bout was the town of Juarez, in Mexico. Johnson was agreeable, and shortly before Christmas, 1914, he commenced his return journey across the Atlantic. In due course he set foot on South American soil at Buenos Aires.

Now, it had been arranged for Johnson to fight Willard in Juarez, but a situation suddenly developed which necessitated a drastic change of plan. While Jack Curley was actually promoting the fight, it was being financed by the fabulous Pancho Villa, the bandit leader and revolutionary who was then the virtual ruler of Mexico. The President of the Republic,

Venustiano Carranza, quite naturally opposed anything sponsored or fostered by Villa, and he announced that he would do his best to stop such a fight from taking place. Jack Johnson said :

    . . . He had the means of stopping it, too, because I could not get into Mexico except by way of Vera Cruz. To have attempted entrance by any other port would have meant my capture and return to the United States, where the prison term awaited me. Carranza declared that if I attempted to land at Vera Cruz, he would make me a prisoner and turn me over to the United States. Confronted by this situation, I got in touch with Curley, who was at Juarez, and suggested that he arrange to have the fight at Havana.*

Pancho Villa withdrew his backing as soon as the Cuban venue was suggested, of course, but Curley contacted two theatrical impresarios, Frazee and Webber, who showed interest in the idea. The upshot was that they agreed to finance the affair, the site of the contest was switched to Havana, and 5 April, 1915, was fixed as the date.

There had been pre-arranged fights before this one and there have been put-up jobs since. Nobody with even a rudimentary knowledge of the machinations connected with such a lucrative form of entertainment as professional boxing would ever seriously attempt to deny it. But whether the holder of the finest money-spinning ace in the whole pugilistic pack of cards – the heavyweight championship of the world – would seriously listen to any inducement to such blatant dishonesty is quite another matter. By 1915 Johnson had reached a point where he was more or less the dictator regarding the financial side of his contests, and so long as he held the title he could command the lion's share of the gate receipts. In addition to this source of revenue there were several no less rich veins of income he could tap. Not the least among them were his personal

* *Jack Johnson – In the Ring – And Out* (National Sports Publishing Co., Chicago, 1927).

appearances on the stage, and he consistently made money for years through his natural ability to strut, pose and spar before the footlights. These bookings, however, depended almost solely upon his retaining the unique position he held : that of the undefeated champion. None knew better than he the true worth of the title, and it is that knowledge which has for so many years caused authorities on boxing to doubt the truth of his statement.

Another factor which might well have led him to ignore any possible suggestion of a faked fight was his overwhelming vanity and his pride in being the world's number one boxer. In fact, it is more than probable that it was only *injured* pride which caused him to explain away his knock-out defeat in the way he did. Gene Tunney, a man who knew what he was talking about, has admitted that there have been 'a few prominent fighters who would rather have the public believe they had been faking than that they tried their best and failed'. He cited Johnson as a particular case and said :

> ... The fact of the matter, as I see it, is that Johnson realised he could not knock out this young fellow or make him quit, so quit himself. Yet he would rather have 'admirers' and fans believe he sold out than that he was all washed up.*

The Negro's word had never at any time in his career been worth relying on : a fact only too well-known among the sporting fraternity, so it is not surprising that his sworn statement was not taken at its face value. When he published the story of his alleged fake again in his autobiography some years later, very little more credence was given to his confession. Throughout the story of his life we are continually brought up against cases where Johnson dishonoured his contracts, promised one thing and then did another, or blatantly embellished certain events in his career and so misrepresented the facts as to make himself appear the injured party or hero in incidents where he was palpably the villain. He was often almost completely irresponsible during the years of his life when he was much in

* Gene Tunney. *A Man Must Fight* (Cape, 1933).

the limelight, and magnificent boxer though he was, it cannot be ignored that as a man he left a great deal to be desired. While the pieces in this book are not primarily concerned with the morals and characters of those individuals whose deeds they recount, Jack Johnson's personal and social life had so great a bearing upon the passing scene of professional boxing during the years between 1908 and 1915 that it is necessary to paint him in his true colours.

Damon Runyon knew Jack Johnson better than most people, and I think he must have been rather surprised when the Negro asked him to contribute an introductory article to the autobiography. Runyon had nothing but praise for Johnson's ring ability, of course, but he felt rather differently about the former champion as a man, and he was far from sure that Johnson would toe the line of complete honesty. He put things as diplomatically as he could; however, I am somewhat astonished that Johnson used Runyon's introduction, particularly the following paragraph :

If he tells the truth, which is doubtful, his will be a most enthralling tale. I say it is doubtful if he tells the truth because John Arthur Johnson isn't old enough to tell the truth in an autobiography. A man has to be just about ready to die before he has the courage of unburdening himself completely.*

Yet although the Johnson-Willard fight has come to be generally accepted as having been won and lost on the merits of the contestants, and many readers may be learning of its dubiety here for the first time, there is still the element of doubt caused by the Negro's sworn affidavit. Although he became a very different man during the second half of his life and came to regret many of the misdeeds and escapades for which he had been responsible, he went to his grave without rescinding his original statement concerning the Havana bout. Johnson must therefore be given a fair hearing, and the facts of the affair from his point of view are as follows :

According to him, Jack Curley told him when arrangements were first made that if he were to lose the fight he could return

* *Jack Johnson – In the Ring – And Out.*

to the United States a free man. It was impressed upon him that both the public and official attitude towards him would change entirely once his hold upon the world's championship was relinquished. The wonder of it all is that Johnson, an astute and experienced man, could ever have believed that the promoters wielded sufficient power to influence the law. If the Negro has been woefully misjudged, and his story is true, he must have been childishly naïve and trusting.

Johnson asserted that upon his arrival in Havana, Curley and his two associates, Frazee and Webber, concluded the arrangements for him to return to the States if he lost the bout, and awarded him sole South American and European rights in the moving pictures as a further inducement to lie down. Apart from the percentage of the gate receipts due to him as his end of the purse, he was to be 'presented' with another lump sum by the backers of Jess Willard for allowing their man to win. The total payment due to him was some $30,000.

He said that his actual fight percentage was paid to him shortly before he left his quarters for the scene of the contest, but that the balance was not forthcoming, with the delay being due to the gate receipts not having been completely counted when the bout commenced. At this stage Johnson did not give evidence of possessing such a trusting nature. According to his story he had agreed to drop for the count in the tenth round, but when that round arrived and his money had still not been paid he remained on his feet until such time as the promised sum was handed to his wife, who sat at the ringside. His admission continues with a statement to the effect that the contest had travelled well past the pre-arranged number of rounds before his money had somehow been scraped together and given to his wife. It was then that she gave him a signal assuring him that it was in her hands and he replied with a nod for her to leave the ringside. In the twenty-sixth round, when, presumably, she had put some distance between herself and the scene of activities, and the possibility of a double-cross had been eliminated as far as he could make it possible, Jack Johnson fulfilled his part of the bargain, took a punch on the jaw and fell on to his back to be counted out.

So goes his version of the affair. He strengthened it by

34

referring to a well-known photograph of the last moments of the contest. This is a widely-published picture which shows him lying on his back with his knees drawn up and with his gloved hands thrown across his face. He stated that this was proof enough of his condition at the time, and that he was perfectly conscious and aware of his surroundings. He held his arms in that position, he insisted, to shield his eyes from the glaring Havana sun, which was beating directly down on to his face. Would a genuinely defeated boxer, a man who had fought for twenty-six rounds against a younger and stronger man, and who had taken a bad beating, be in possession enough of his senses, after taking a knock-out punch, to concern himself with the sun's rays?

Let us examine the facts and weigh the evidence he offers in the photograph. Firstly, while there is no doubt that his arms were thrown up, the shadow they cast did not fall upon his eyes but upon his brow and chin. While admitting that the split-second exposure may have been made while his arms and gloves were still moving towards the position he may have intended, it was Johnson himself, and nobody else, who proffered this dubious photograph as evidence. Secondly, the possibility of his position being nothing more than a reflex action is a suggestion that was made at the time and which was recalled many years later – in 1946, to be precise – when another heavyweight championship fight ended with one of the contestants being counted out in an almost identical posture. Billy Conn, the defeated boxer, did not excuse himself on the grounds that the powerful lamps above the ring were affecting his eyes and that he threw up his arms to shade them; he did not, in fact, seek to explain his defeat in any other manner than to admit that he was knocked out in a perfectly fair fight and that his conqueror, Joe Louis, was overwhelmingly the better man.*

What, then, of the indisputable evidence of Jack Johnson's wife leaving the ringside shortly before the end? Quite as feasible as the Negro's story is the one, offered by witnesses of the bout, that Johnson knew he was tiring, knew that he could not last much longer, knew that his tenure of the championship

* Ironically, Johnson was killed in a car crash near Raleigh, North Carolina, while on his way to New York to witness this very contest!

was reaching its end, and so instructed his wife to leave in order that she might be spared the ordeal of seeing him floored and beaten.

Johnson boasted that he could have stopped Willard long before he himself went down, had the fight been a straight one. He would have us believe that he was still getting the better of things until the final punch. Yet the film shows him taking a systematic and gruelling beating in the later stages, and the reports from the experts who sat within a few feet of the pair credit Willard with having delivered heavy punishment. The very last punches, those which sent Johnson crashing to the canvas, knocked two of his famous golden teeth down his throat. When he fell, Jack Johnson was not unconscious, but there is not much doubt that he could never have arisen within the prescribed ten seconds.

A brief summary of the whole fight would suggest that for close on twenty rounds Johnson easily had the better of the exchanges, and that despite his poor physical condition and his opponent's extreme fitness, they were poles apart in the matter of sheer boxing ability. But Johnson could not seriously hurt the gigantic Willard, who was quite content to play a waiting game. So disinclined was the challenger to force matters that when Johnson tired and refused to lead or set the pace, the bout became very dull and both men sparred for long periods without attempting to land telling punches. After a few rounds of this sort, during which the champion became more fatigued and breathless with each succeeding minute, Willard began to assert himself. Concentrating on the body, the big cowboy hinted that the end was near during the twenty-fifth round. On answering the bell for the next session, Willard immediately crowded his man and launched an attack which suggested that he had received instructions to go for a knock-out. This offensive was too much for the coloured fighter, now dog-tired and with his wind gone, and when the challenger administered the *coup de grâce* and knocked Johnson down, the fallen man was too far gone to get up again.

The known facts of this extraordinary battle now having been offered, it is up to the reader to weigh the evidence and decide for himself whether Jack Johnson sold his championship, and told the truth about it, whether he was knocked out

36

and refused to give his conqueror credit, or whether he had had enough and called it a day by dropping for the count and later sought to excuse his apparently fully-conscious state on the canvas by concocting the frame-up story.

As for the full story of the title fight : the detailed description of the battle's highlights, it lacked a great many of the thrills and knock-downs often in evidence in heavyweight title affairs, despite the contest having been the longest championship meeting ever decided with gloves in this particular division. But the essential facts concerning the bout and the principals are as follows :

Jess Willard was not a natural pugilist. At first he had no aptitude for the game and no particular liking for it. But in 1910, after Johnson had defeated the hitherto invincible Jim Jeffries, the whole world went slightly mad looking for a White Hope. Managers and so-called talent-spotters scoured the whole of the United States looking for a potential world-beater. Farmers, cowboys, miners and labourers were all inveigled into taking to the ring for a living, provided they were big enough : over six feet and upwards of fourteen stone. Most of them fell by the wayside after one or two disastrous fights, but a few of the bigger and better-tutored ones showed a little promise. Willard was perhaps not the best, but he was certainly the biggest. Standing six feet six and scaling something like sixteen-and-a-half stone, he was lured from the Kansas plains where he worked as a cowboy and was dubbed the Tall Pine of Pottawatomie. For such a giant, he couldn't punch anything like his weight, and there was nothing pugnacious about him at all. Added to this, he was inclined to be lazy, and he hated training, but persistent conditioners and coaches instilled into him the basic moves of boxing, and after a time he began to develop a pretty useful orthodox attack and defence. Prodding out his long straight-left, he won most of his fights simply because smaller men just couldn't get near him.

He had never been knocked out, but two White Hopes with more natural aptitude for their chosen profession, Luther McCarthy and Gunboat Smith, had shown up his deficiencies in 'no decision contests', and by 1915 he was just another

37

false alarm in the campaign to find a man to beat Jack Johnson. How was it, then, that he, of all boxers, should have been the man chosen to meet the Negro for the championship of the world?

The simple truth of the matter is that big Jess Willard was just then about the best bet among a pretty poor bunch. Gunboat Smith had blotted his copy-book by being beaten in London on a foul by a light-heavyweight, Georges Carpentier, who had now gone to war. He followed up this disaster by losing to Sam Langford, a Negro reputed by some to be as good as Johnson. Luther McCarthy had died accidentally after a first-round punch from Arthur Pelkey, who in turn had been knocked out by Smith. The only other big fellow with any pretensions to world championship class, Frank Moran, had had his chance against Johnson in Paris, in 1914, and had lost. So it had to be Jess Willard or nobody.

Jack Johnson weighed in at fourteen stone nine-and-a-half pounds, more than half a stone heavier than when he had won the championship in 1908. Willard tipped the beam at sixteen stone six pounds, and thus began the fight with an advantage of twenty-four-and-a-half pounds. About 20,000 people paid to see the contest, but many more witnessed it from the distance of the low hills bordering the Oriental Park course. The gate receipts did not even approach the figures set up in many far less important non-championship promotions in America and Britain both before and since. The defending title-holder's guarantee swallowed up almost all of the purse, and Willard received little more than his training expenses for the opportunity of boxing for the world's title. The referee was Jack Welsh, the ringside betting odds were at about 8–5 in the Negro's favour, and for some reason never satisfactorily explained by the promoters the first round did not commence until an hour after the scheduled time. It must be admitted that this delay certainly lends credence to Johnson's story about his bunce being not forthcoming at the start of the contest. It also caused many wild rumours and apprehensions among the audience which were dispelled the moment the boxers entered the sunlit ring.

38

Jack Johnson was seen to be carrying quite a lot of unnecessary flesh on his body, particularly about the waist-line. Although the fight was not limited to the twenty rounds then in vogue for important contests, and there was always the possibility of its going much longer, Johnson had made no real attempt to get himself into condition. This *could* have been because he knew he was throwing the fight, but it could also have been because he had lived pretty high off the hog since 1911. The fat accumulated over several years is not easily disposed of in a few months. On the other hand, Jess Willard had made preparations far more intensive than at any other time in his career. Those in charge of his training had known that the Tall Pine of Pottawatomie stood little chance of winning quickly, and they had concentrated on bringing their man into the ring fit enough to endure the longest and most punishing of battles. It is arguable that the lazy Willard would never have submitted himself to such an arduous grind for a fight he knew was fixed in his favour: it is just as arguable that his ever-ready sponsors had taken into consideration the possibility of a double-cross by the wily Johnson, and had adopted reasonable precautions. Certainly Willard had trained for a marathon race rather than for a boxing-match, and on the face of things he set out from the first bell to wait until the coloured title-holder began to show signs of distress.

Johnson did all the leading for the first hour. He was so much more skilful than his gigantic but raw opponent that he landed almost at will. While they were at long range the smaller man scored points with ridiculous ease, but when they came together Willard leaned heavily on Johnson to tire him. Occasionally he would bring in powerful but ponderous blows to the body, and although at first Johnson did not seem at all distressed by these punches, their cumulative effect began to tell in time.

After ten rounds both men seemed to be going strongly, but although the champion had connected countless times with his deliveries to the head and body, he appeared unable to stagger Willard or even to cause him an anxious moment. The knowledge that he was fighting a big man whom he could not hurt seemed to occur to Johnson during the interval after the eleventh round, for he came out of his corner for the next session in a desperate manner. The twelfth and thirteenth rounds were the fastest, the most thrilling and the most varied, for Johnson showed everything he knew. (Could it have been that since his money hadn't arrived by round ten – when he had agreed to take the dive – he then suspected that he might be being double-crossed?)

These two rounds were so one-sided that it was almost laughable. Willard looked as if he were taking a terrific beating, yet all he did was to smile. When the Negro stalked him in the thirteenth round and twice whipped home a smashing right to the point of the jaw, his challenger just shook his head and carried on. Both punches would have floored and beaten any ordinary heavyweight.

Now Willard began to show more activity. It must have been dreadful for Jack Johnson to know that he had done everything in his power to drop his opponent, only to have him coming back in a manner which suggested that he was indestructible. For the first time in the battle things were not quite so one-sided, but the champion was still good enough to take the major honours in each round. He began to talk to Willard and to jest at his expense with the ringsiders, but there was a very different reason behind his comments from that which had led him to taunt opponents in his younger days. Then he had been brash and cocky, out to humiliate the whites who had kept him subjugated for so long, but now he was aiming verbal thrusts at Willard in an attempt to ruffle his man and cause him to fight wildly and leave himself open. But Johnson's remarks went right over Willard's head. The big fellow had his plan of campaign and nothing would shift him from it.

The wise betting had now switched in favour of Willard, but still the majority of onlookers felt that the champion might save the day. The cheers and yells from the many coloured members of the crowd were mostly in his favour. Yet by the twentieth round even his most staunch supporters must, like himself, have seen the writing on the wall. At this point in the fight Johnson ceased leading with his left and dropped all attempts to set the pace. He now made it quite clear that Willard must come to him.

But the challenger was still not ready to launch his offensive, and for about four rounds the contest grew extremely dull and slow. Johnson's body was gleaming with sweat and he was breathing heavily. It was clear that he could not carry on like this much longer. All during the twenty-fifth he showed more interest in his wife at the ringside than in the fight, and shortly before the bell ended the round his tall adversary suddenly walked in with a tremendous right to the body while Johnson's attentions were elsewhere. It was the best punch of the battle, and it almost finished the Negro. His knees buckled, his eyes rolled, and he grimaced in pain. He fell into a clinch and hung on until the bell came to his rescue.

While he sat in his corner during the interval he gave the signal for his wife to leave, which she did, and then began the round which was to prove to be the last. Johnson got up from his stool when the bell rang, but he was still so affected by the punch he had taken that he made no move to come forward and meet Willard. The referee had to beckon him in, but his opponent hopped across the ring quickly and now launched his first real sustained attack of the contest. He must have been advised that the time was ripe for going in, and he followed his instructions to the letter. He never ceased throwing lefts and rights at the wilting Negro, and although a few rounds earlier Johnson might have slipped them with ease he was now far too tired to even block them. Willard rained blows on his head and jaw and forced him round and round the ring. Then suddenly, after a minute or so, the big man switched his attack to the body and succeeded in landing a murderous right to the stomach. It was the decisive punch, and it knocked what little fight there remained in the champion right out of him. His hands came down, and with them his head. Willard slammed in two more punches to the face and jaw and Jack Johnson went down, flat on his back and almost on the edge of the ring. Then he drew up his knees, raised his arms over his face, and was counted out in the much-discussed position.

After Willard was announced the victor, a riot broke out among the onlookers. Hundreds of Cubans, who had bet heavily on Johnson for no sounder reason than that he was coloured like themselves, now turned against the beaten man and sought to molest him. But precautions had been taken before the fight, and the scene was patrolled by a small army of police and soldiers. These forces now surrounded the ring and safely escorted Johnson to his dressing-room. He was well-protected from any harm and he reached his hotel safely, where he told the press that he had been beaten by the heat and his lack of condition. It was some weeks later before he made his first statement regarding collusion. Willard's purported comment, made after he had heard that Johnson had stated that he had deliberately lost, was as follows: 'If Johnson throwed that fight, I wish he throwed it sooner. It was hotter than hell down there.'

The end of the coloured champion's reign inevitably brought to a close the long search for a White Hope, and it also rang down the curtain upon an extremely fascinating and eventful pugilistic era. But it did not end the career of Jack Johnson. He fought a number of recorded contests against second-class opposition and was still occasionally boxing ten years after he lost the title. Official records show his last bout as having been decided in 1924, but his own compilation of the summary of his career lists contests during 1926, when he was approaching the age of fifty. Although he would have us believe that even then he was good enough to box his way back to the heights and regain his championship, the men he met were far removed from the top shelf.

Jack Johnson did not surrender himself to the United States authorities immediately after the Willard fight, as he had half intended to do, since, as he said:

... I found that such offers of leniency as had been tendered were without substantial foundation, and that immediate prospects for my return to my own country without going to prison were so slight that I could not give them serious thought.*

He returned to Europe, and for some time he settled in the neutral territory of Spain. Here he capitalised on his reputation with a brief appearance as a matador, and later he turned

* *Jack Johnson – In the Ring – And Out.*

to professional wrestling. He boxed once or twice and secured occasional stage engagements, and then, when the United States entered the war, in 1917, he acted as a sort of intelligence agent for the country from which he was still a fugitive. Most of his operations were confined to watching the activities of German submarines off the coast of Spain, and I suspect that they were probably self-imposed. In 1919 he returned to Mexico, and after several months in Tia Juana – the nearest he could get to the States while still remaining abroad – he made up his mind to surrender himself and take what punishment was due to him. The upshot was that in 1920 Johnson was confined to Leavenworth Penitentiary to serve his term of a year and a day.

Because of good behaviour during his sentence, Johnson shortened his stay in prison to eight months, and during that time he did more boxing and training than anything else. He was put in charge of the physical direction of the other inmates, and apart from the fact that he was confined within the walls of the building and was therefore, technically, a prisoner, it was not nearly so difficult an ordeal as he had imagined it would be.

He left Leavenworth a free man with the liberty to travel anywhere in the United States for the first time since his hasty exit from that country several years before, and the Negro picked up his life of itinerant adventure, boxing here and there, making money and losing it, until he was too old to make a living with his fists. It was then that Johnson really began to feel the pinch, and before his violent death in 1946 in a car accident he was more than once reduced to living in near poverty.

Although at one time he appeared in a crowd scene in an opera on the New York stage and was unrecognised by many of those in the audience, and on another occasion he is said to have worked with a flea circus, his name as a boxer was never forgotten, and his deeds during the heyday of his career still continue to occupy space in the various sporting publications throughout the world. Of course, it is impossible to assess, with any degree of accuracy, which champion was the greatest of all, but it is the opinion of most of those experts who saw each of those old 'uns in his prime that Jack Johnson, first

43

coloured holder of the heavyweight championship of the world, was also the peer of them all within the ropes.

5   No Decision

If you are a reader of American boxing record books and are in the habit of looking up the old-time fighters you will frequently come up against the abbreviation N.D. These letters are as common, if not commoner, than the letters K.O. in the records of a great many pugilists. Now, whereas the dumbest reader very soon realises that K.O. is short for knock-out, if he didn't already know it, N.D. is not so readily construed as being short for 'no decision', even by the brightest of the uninitiated. But once the code has been broken, the trouble does not end there. What exactly does no decision mean?

It means that the particular boxer one is reading about in the records plied his trade during an era when the business was, strictly speaking, illegal in certain states of the American union. Authority had decided that for two men to come together and box a *contest,* one to be adjudged the winner over the other, was unlawful. You could be heavily fined or even go to prison if you flouted the law.

The people, however, easily got round this unpleasant legislation – as is usually the case with unpopular laws. They soon found that there was nothing on the statute books to prevent two young athletes from coming together to demonstrate an *exhibition* of the noble art of fisticuffs, as long as no arbiter announced after it was all over that one or the other was a winner. A referee was employed to keep order within the ring, or course, but had he publicly declared that one man had bested the other, then this spirited exhibition of sparring would automatically have been reduced to nothing more than a brutal prize-fight, and would have been illegal.

Naturally, now and again things grew rather too hectic in these brisk exhibitions, and one of the participants would take quite a pasting. In the event of such an unanticipated occurrence the referee would quite rightly halt proceedings. Again, it was not entirely unknown for one athlete to run rather violently against the other's fist during the exchanges, and to be so stunned as to find it difficult to continue the exhibition, and be obliged to seek respite upon the floor of the ring. Should he recline there for more than ten seconds it would be plainly obvious to all concerned that he was in no condition to resume, and the whole affair would then be terminated. During happenings of this sort, of course, no official decision was needed anyway.

But what of those bouts that went the full distance of six, eight or ten rounds? How could an honest citizen of a sporting tendency who was desirous of wagering a dollar or two on the outcome indulge his innocent fun as he had done in earlier and happier days? And how could the average citizen, quite understandably interested in the fluctuating waxings and wanings of the prowess of those exhibitionists involved, arrive at some sort of conclusion? Quite simply : he had only to look at the following morning's newspapers.

While it was strictly illegal for any referee or ringside panel of judges to announce one man as the winner over another, there was no law which said that a sports reporter could not pass an opinion. Naturally, on occasion, particularly when the arts, crafts and skills of both athletes were fairly evenly demonstrated, one newspaper might reasonably declare that boxer A had displayed his to the better advantage, and another newspaper might, equally reasonably, support the talents of boxer B. In order to avoid such an outcome, any citizen with a sporting tendency was obliged to abide by a particular newspaper's opinion before any bookmaker would take his bet.

This sort of thing was all right as far as it went. But itinerant professional boxers would, quite understandably, collect the cuttings from those papers which flattered them and forget all about those reports which didn't. Arriving in a new town, and looking up the local promoter for a possible engagement, their recent records listing a long string of N.D.s would mean nothing at all. Promoters very soon learned to take the newspaper cutting evidence with a pinch of salt and fell back upon relying on their own judgment.

The 'no decision' business also encouraged laziness on the part of big-name pugs and champions. Champions, in particular, had quite a time of it. They could pick up considerable purse money by confining their activities to those states which did not allow decisions, and by waltzing through six or ten rounds in the confident knowledge that provided they could avoid being caught by a knock-out punch their reputations were safe. Local newspapers might unanimously report that they had been outpointed, and bets would be decided on these opinions, but the record books would list these particular bouts with the two letters N.D.

One of the cleverest featherweights who ever lived was a Welshman named Jim Driscoll. Many British sports enthusiasts who have read about this phenomenal boxer have oftened wondered, quite reasonably, why he was never recognised as champion of the world, if he was all that good. The answer lies in the age in which he lived. Driscoll flourished during the first decade of the twentieth century, which was also a heyday of the 'no decision' vogue in the States. Featherweight champion of the world was a remarkable little Jew from San Francisco named Abe Attell, and partisan *aficionados* across the water have named him the best of all time at his weight. Now, in late 1908 and early 1909, Jim Driscoll spent some four months in the United States, and he boxed ten times. Three times he appeared in Boston, in the state of Massachusetts, where they allowed decisions, and he won handily on each occasion. He boxed three times in Philadelphia, in the state of Pennsylvania, where they did not allow decisions, and these three engagements are listed N.D. Two of these were versus Grover Hayes, a very good man, and the fact that Driscoll outpointed him well in one of his Boston fights suggests the way the other ones went. The other four bouts took place in New York City, in another state where no decision was allowed. One of his opponents, the last in a triumphant tour, as it happened, was Abe Attell, who was cute enough not to get caught boxing so formidable an opponent outside 'no decision' territory. Once again we find N.D. against this meeting in the record books, but that eminent ring historian, Nat Fleischer, appends an asterisk against this listing in his own compilation. That asterisk informs us : 'Driscoll easily best'. The Welshman outpointed Abe Attell on 19 February, 1909, and virtually took his world's title away from him. He definitely proved, as far I am concerned, that he was the best featherweight in the world, if nothing else.

One of the most active lightweights who ever boxed was Benny Leonard. His career extended from 1912 until 1924, by which time he had fought himself right out of opposition at his poundage and so retired undefeated champion of the world. (He did come back for about a year in the early Thirties, to try and recoup a fortune lost in the stock market crash, but this disaster can be discounted.)

Leonard is remembered as something of a marvel. For most of his career he boxed two or three times a month, and sometimes oftener, usually in New York, Pennsylvania, or the other eastern states. For practically the whole of this time he boxed 'no decision' contests, and he faced some pretty good men. Between 1914 and 1922 he opposed, among others, the following 'name' fighters: Pal Moore, Johnny Dundee, Johnny Kilbane, Rocky Kansas, Freddy Welsh, Jack Britton, Ted 'Kid' Lewis, Soldier Bartfield and Lew Tendler. Six of these boxers, at some time or another, were world's champions themselves, at featherweight, lightweight or welterweight. Some of them Leonard faced two or three times. On one occasion he most definitely knocked out Welsh to win his lightweight title, and on another he was most emphatically bested by Britton, before fouling his way out of the match. These particular contests, because they came to a decisive conclusion, are now remembered. But what about the 'no decision' affairs Leonard fought with Welsh and Britton, and all those other bouts with the above-listed boxers, which have gone down in the records with an enigmatical N.D.? Who won them, Benny Leonard? We would have to delve into the archives of the local American newspapers of the time to get a clue.

6   Pet Punches

It would be an exaggeration to say that every boxer has a pet punch, or a special delivery, as it were. But it is certainly a fact that almost every man who ever gains any great notoriety or popularity in the ring sooner or later becomes known for his successful execution of a particular blow. Among the so-called Fancy Dans, those speedy, long-range, orthodox practitioners of their art, the classic left-lead is, of course, the most common. These men firmly believe that the shortest distance between two points is a straight line, and they usually lead, or take the initiative in the exchanges. The more rugged gentry, oftener than not inclined towards robustness and physical power, tend to wait until the other fellow leads and then counter with shorter, hooked blows, which add to their destructiveness because the recipient is usually coming in on to them.

This, of course, is something of the theory of boxing at its most basic and elemental. Between the two extremes of style and approach there is an infinite variety of permutations. As outstanding examples of individuals who couldn't be pigeonholed there was the great Ray Robinson, a lanky stylist whose physique appeared to demand that he should never mix things with a brawler, but who was nothing short of lethal when he elected to go in and finish a fight; and, strange as it may seem, the equally great Henry Armstrong, a man whose almost unvarying tactics were to present the top of his head and his brow to an opponent and then to start punching with hooks, jabs and uppercuts from bell to bell. The fastest and cleverest boxers in the world could do little with him : he never let them get set. Master point-scorers were usually too busy defending themselves to be able to chalk up many marks on the offensive. Yet although Armstrong stopped a great many opponents during his career, this was by virtue of the cumulative effect of his blows rather than their weight. Contrary to popular belief, Armstrong was not a particularly heavy puncher. Had he been, no fighter of his time could ever have lived with him for more than a round or two.

I suppose the left-lead, or jab, must be the most commonly-used blow in pugilism. I never saw anybody utilise it with more punishing effect than Joe Louis, although he was not the type to dance round the ring and streak in and out on twinkling toes. He tended to box on the flat of his feet, and he rarely moved them more than an inch or two as he jabbed out that left glove into an opponent's face. Although he finished most of his fights with a right-hand knock-out punch, it was that short, damaging jab which usually paved the way. A contemporary of mine once said that he would always remember Louis from those countless ringside photos which used to appear in the boxing magazines during the Thirties and Forties : on the floor of the ring lies or sits a stricken opponent; on the way to a neutral corner, head down, and usually in back view, lopes the Brown Bomber. This aspect of Louis is, without doubt, the commonest in existence, but for my own part I shall always recall him, poker-faced and completely concentrated, with his feet close together and his gloves held high, ready to poke out that amazing left-jab.

The classic straight-left, rarely seen today as it used to be delivered, should streak out towards an opponent with the simultaneous stepping forward of a pace with the left foot. Correctly employed, it has far more effect than the jab. We are told that Jim Driscoll was a master of its execution, and I can well believe it. Unfortunately, he was before my time, and I have never even seen him on film. I have been luckier with one or two others who made a speciality of this blow. Tommy Loughran, in his days as light-heavyweight champion, in the nineteen-twenties, seemed to me to exemplify that overworked expression : poetry in motion. He really was a delight to watch. Don't miss the film of his fifteen rounds against Leo Lomski, for instance, if ever you are offered the chance to watch it. Loughran's tragedy was that he went on too long. Financial needs obliged him to step into the heavyweight class to box men much bigger and stronger than himself. In the twilight of his long career he was often beaten by men who would never have been allowed in the same ring with him ten years earlier. Yet he was still clever enough to avoid getting badly hurt.

Bombardier Wells was another straight-left artist who was a pleasure to watch. It had been pointed out elsewhere that his defeats gained far more publicity than his victories. This is true,

49

and for that reason I suppose he will always be remembered as something of a disappointment, succumbing to the big punch on the big occasions. Yet in a busy career lasting over fifteen years no man ever won a points decision over him. For that matter, no man ever looked like outpointing him. He had a long and accurate straight-left, the like of which had seldom been seen in a heavyweight. More, he didn't just tap with it. There was more than fourteen stone of bone and muscle behind it every time he shot it out. After a round or two of absorbing punches of this calibre full in the face, most of his adversaries began to wonder why they had ever adopted such a means of livelihood. He softened up and completely outclassed so many opponents with that battering ram of a straight-left that in almost fifty fights Wells was taken the full distance to a referee's verdict only twice. Unhappily he couldn't absorb a really stiff dig himself, although he was game enough. Time and again he had his man groggy and reeling from his methodical barrage, only to walk into just one desperately-thrown punch and fall for the full count.

Departing from the masters of the straight-left, there were a host of fighters who gained a reputation by the use of pet blows a little less orthodox and fundamental. One of them was a big former dentist from Pittsburgh named Frank Moran, who flourished during the Jack Johnson era. It is said that his explanation for deserting a sedentary occupation for a manual one was that he 'found it easier to knock teeth out than pull 'em out.' It is a good story, but my admittedly limited experience of Moran in action – films of his two world's title challenges versus Johnson and Willard – leads me to believe that he found his new method of extraction anything but easy. Moran had a right-hand punch, which he christened Mary Ann : he literally had nothing else. His unvarying tactic was to approach an opponent, hold out his left arm as a sort of measuring rod, and then hurl over his right in a blind swipe at the jaw. Nine times out of ten his opposite number saw it coming and avoided it completely. Occasionally it landed somewhere on an arm or shoulder, his man backed away, and Moran got a second shot. Most of those missed, too, but on rare occasions Mary Ann did connect with a temple or jawbone, and down went the owner.

Frank Moran had two chances at the heavyweight championship of the world, which, on the face of things, would suggest that he was something fairly special. The true fact is that, barring Mary Ann, he was not. He was in the world's title class simply because, at that time, competition was limited. Jack Johnson accepted him as a challenger at a time when he, the champion, was fat and untrained and knew that all he had to do was avoid Mary Ann. He avoided it for twenty rounds. Bill Brady, who reported this fight from Paris for an American newspaper, summed up Moran thus : 'The poor boy doesn't know what his hands are for.' A couple of years later Jess Willard, who had beaten Johnson in the interim, consented to face Moran in a ten rounds 'no decision' fight, which meant that the challenger had to do his damnest to win by a knock-out while the champion only needed to avoid it in order to retain his title. I don't think the famous Mary Ann connected once during the whole fight – if fight we can really call it. The bigger Willard just fobbed-off the willing-enough Moran for ten monotonous rounds and took no chances at all. It has been said of this contest that the only person in any danger at all was the referee, who was constantly exposed to the possibility of contracting pneumonia from the draughts and other insidious currents of air caused by the passing of Frank Moran's highly-touted Mary Ann. Old John L. Sullivan, at that time an elderly and white-bewhiskered, paunchy gentleman who had been invited to witness this contest for the championship he had once so proudly held, had this to say : 'If that was a fight I just saw, then I challenge both of the bums right now.'

As regards a very different sort of punch, I am reminded of one of the first world champions to come to Great Britain after the war, ready to defend his title against a native challenger. He was a well-muscled American Negro lightweight named Ike Williams. We knew very little about him over here at the time, apart from the fact that he was a champion at his weight and therefore must be no slouch. But he was to meet Ronnie James, the British lightweight title-holder, a Welsh stylist of whom we thought a great deal. The war years had put a stop to most serious international competition, and it was felt that James had marked time, awaiting his chance, for long enough.

51

The consensus of opinion was that Ronnie James stood a fifty-fifty chance of lifting the world's lightweight crown from the head of the little-known Ike Williams, and he certainly looked good in the opening rounds. Boxing before a Welsh crowd in Cardiff, he more than held his own for better than half the scheduled fifteen rounds. It was then that Ike Williams really went to work.

Having lulled James into a false sense of security, and having shown nothing at all of world's championship class, he came out for round nine with no immediate promise of revealing anything extraordinary. But he suddenly stepped in and whipped a right to the body which dropped Ronnie James as though he had been shot. Nobody in the stadium had ever seen a blow like it before. It had begun from somewhere near Williams's own right shoulder. The blow had moved backwards and downwards in an arc, and had then moved forward in a vicious dig to the liver. Its impact was devastating. James got up from it, it is true, only to go down again and again from similar deliveries to the self-same spot. He had no reply to the punch and no defence against it.

In the following morning's paper we learned that Wales had witnessed the dreaded 'bolo' punch. It has been said that there is nothing new under the sun. Certainly this particular blow had been in use for many years before Ike Williams threw it at Cardiff, but I, for one, cannot recall having seen it employed before.

The left-hook is a punch which, over the years, has brought considerable success to those who could use it properly. Correctly delivered, it can have a paralysing effect, either to the jaw or to the body. At its best, it is short and fast, usually essayed at relatively close quarters. For this reason, an uninitiated watcher could easily miss its execution entirely, while the more spectacular long right-handers tend to catch the eye. As an example, take that short but dramatic film of the famous Dempsey-Firpo fight. All the action and fireworks seem to come from the enormous so-called Wild Bull of the Pampas. He is on the aggressive perpetually, and while he is erect his arms seem never to stop moving. But it is Dempsey who scores all the clean punches, and almost all of the knock-downs.

What happened was that Luis Angel Firpo, an untutored

young giant of a man, came out of his corner like the wild bull he had been dubbed and started throwing his right from almost half way across the ring, while he was still well out of distance. He threw himself after it, too, and the very first punch happened to land. It clubbed Dempsey to his knees, but he was up in the fraction of a second, and retaliated with short hooks which quite literally travelled only a matter of inches before they found their mark. They almost pole-axed Firpo. The brief battle which followed was so exciting that the whole vast crowd came to its feet with a roar, and many of the thousands watching had no clear idea, either then or in retrospect, just what actually went on. Wrote Thomas Wolfe, years later :

That was no fight, no scheduled contest for a title. It was a burning point in time, a kind of concentration of our total energies, of the blind velocity of the period, cruel, ruthless, savage, swift, bewildering as America. The fight, thus seen, resumed and focalised a period in the nation's life. It lasted six minutes. It was over almost before it had begun. In fact, the spectators had no sense of its beginning. It exploded there before them.*

Dempsey had no recollection of the first round. Robbed of his consciousness in the very first exchange, he fought back by instinct, but he fought in such a way that his short, unspectacular hooks smashed Firpo to the boards for a count almost every time they landed properly. Years of disciplined training, together with that natural left-hook, demonstrated how the genius of a great champion can overcome the blind and brute, bludgeoning force of apparently overwhelming physical odds. Still, I do not deny that luck was on his side. After dropping the fight-mad and seemingly indestructible Firpo no fewer than seven times in that unique first round, with punches hardly anybody present actually saw, he was forced to the ropes, took a swipe which was half a punch and half a push, and hurtled backwards head first out of the ring and on to the bodies of the reporters. Several pairs of hands and arms, only too willing to do the job, pushed and levered him back into the ring,

* Thomas Wolfe. *The Web and the Rock* (Heinemann, 1947).

shortly before the bell ended the most dramatic round in boxing history.

Sitting in his corner, Dempsey was jerked into awareness by smelling-salts and the desperate ministrations of his seconds. 'What round coming up?' he asked.

'Second,' replied his manager, Jack Kearns.

Now began the round that proved to be the last. If Luis Firpo's punches may be likened to the blows of a piledriver, then Dempsey's hooks were delivered like a man driving home rivets. Thus Thomas Wolfe once more :

> ... The killer had learned caution now. He came out craftily this time, with his black jaw tucked in below his shoulder. It was all over then. The great bull had no weapons for methods such as these. He lowered his head and charged. The riveter shot him down.*

Dempsey's hook was christened Iron Mike, and it was the most famous punch of its era. Long after the spring and energy had gone from his legs and he no longer retained the wind to carry him through a fight of long duration he could still embark upon a series of barnstorming tours against young hopefuls in four-round 'exhibitions' and dump his luckless and surprised opponents on to their backs for the count with that amazing left-hook.

Much more recently, the most widely-publicised punch of this nature, I suppose, is that of Henry Cooper. Everyone has heard of 'Enery's 'Ammer, and he never employed it to better advantage than in his first encounter with Cassius Clay. He whipped that demolishing left-hook across to the jaw in the closing seconds of the fourth round, and deposited the most valuable piece of pugilistic property in the world on to the seat of its pants. Clay got up from it, it is true, but he also got up from it far too quickly, either because of the indignity of being floored or because he simply didn't know what was going on. I believe that there is not the slightest doubt that Clay would have been knocked out a second or two later had not the bell rung for the end of the round, but I also believe that far too much attention has been paid to that knock-down.

* *The Web and the Rock.*

Clay came out for the fifth round and proceeded to so outclass Cooper with a dazzling exhibition of speed and boxing that I think he might well have scored a knock-out himself in the next few moments had not the referee intervened to save the Englishman from too much punishment to a badly-cut eyebrow.

Now Henry Cooper is an extremely likeable fellow, and he is deservedly popular for his efforts in bringing British boxing out of a lean period. But – and I know this is sheer heresy – I think his continued position as one of the leading contenders for the heavyweight championship of the world flattered him, 'Enery's 'Ammer notwithstanding. Although he boxed Cassius Clay twice, on the second occasion for the title, he was never really in the same category or class, as a pugilist, as the phenomenal coloured man. The near knock-out he scored in their first bout was not actually a lucky punch, but it would never have landed had Clay not been stalling and boxing his way desultorily towards the fulfilment of his predictory rhyme : 'It ain't no jive, he falls in five.' When they met the second time, of course, the whole world watched and listened for Cooper to connect again with that famous left-hook. He did not do so. He did not even look like landing it. Although this contest ended unsatisfactorily, again with Cooper's brow badly cut, I am perfectly sure that there could have been no other ending but a victory for the champion.

If the supporters of Henry Cooper continue to insist that he was just unlucky in not defeating Clay, and was as good a man, barring accidents, I would refer them to a fight which took place shortly afterwards : Cooper versus Floyd Patterson. The old world champion was something of a veteran at the time, and engaged upon one of his numerous come-back efforts to fight his way to the top of the heap again. He was a left-hook artist himself, although 'Enery's 'Ammer overshadowed his own speciality. When the crunch eventually came, in the fourth round, it was Patterson's left-hook, not Cooper's, which triumphed. Henry Cooper was knocked cold, as decisively beaten as any fighter could possibly be.

Floyd Patterson will not, I think, be remembered as one of the greatest of all heavyweight champions. He took a terrible beating from Ingemar Johansson, which stemmed from a powerful right-hander which later became known in this country as Ingo's Bingo, and he put up two inglorious displays in opposition to the much bigger and stronger Sonny Liston. But never forget that he was the first man in boxing history to regain the heavyweight championship of the world. He accomplished this unique feat with the execution of the finest left-hook I have ever seen in my life. It caught Ingemar Johansson on the point of the jaw in the fifth round and stretched him unconscious. Johansson didn't move a muscle during the count. Patterson's tragedy was that he was rather small for a heavyweight and, his own powerful punch notwithstanding, couldn't take a really heavy blow himself when facing a bigger man.

7 Apocryphal – I

Some of the best stories and anecdotes of the ring have only the minimum of fact as a basis. I believe that most of them germinated in the minds of astute press agents and/or newspapermen.

Boxing is a colourful enough occupation in itself, without embellishment. In its literature tall stories and eccentricities abound, and these tend to make the profession appear more colourful than ever.

Certain dumb clucks who attained a considerable notoriety in the past by virtue of a pair of willing fists or a wild private life while they were in the money must have been slightly outraged, at the start of their careers, to read in the papers – or more probably have it brought to their attention by those who could read papers – that they had said or done certain things. But later, in company with people like film stars and prominent politicians, they grew blasé about what was said of them or what was written about them in the press. In some cases, provided the reportage was flattering enough, they even grew to believe that some of the events related really happened. In other cases – and I am by no means referring to dumb clucks here – the subjects just laughed it all off. But those stories 'growed'. They growed and growed year by year, and those concerned must have raised some very overworked eyebrows whenever they noted the latest absurdities.

To cite a particular case : Young Griffo was an extraordinarily fast and elusive lightweight who flourished during the last decade of the nineteenth century. He was born in Sydney, New South Wales, and he served his apprenticeship exclusively in Australian rings, where he was reasonably successful without actually creating a sensation. You will find one or two knock-out victories interspersed among the wins and draws of his early record, but they were all against unknown men. His talents did not lie in the direction of hard-hitting, and even after he sailed for the United States in the summer of 1893 until the end of his career some ten years later he is credited with having scored only one knock-out in about fifty contests.

Now Griffo was active at a period in pugilism when the ring was full of men who might be termed today as some pretty tough cookies. Among others, he faced George Dixon, Jack McAuliffe, Kid Lavigne and Joe Gans, all world champions at one time or another. Griffo did not defeat a single one of these men, although he did gain the distinction of having boxed draws with three of them. Young Griffo is remembered as an extremely slippery customer who was not only hard to beat but very hard to hit.

After he had seen his best days, it was said that he made a habit of going into saloons, spreading a handkerchief on the floor and inviting anyone present to try and knock him off it. He didn't do this for fun, of course. It seems that he put himself up as a human coconut-shy in order to earn himself a few cents to buy a drink.

Griffo retained an on-the-spot elusiveness well after his active ring days when the spring had gone out of his legs, and I have no doubt that he earned himself many a slug of whisky by ducking and dodging the blows of the ham-fisted gentry who frequented the American saloons. He *must* have done so, since from all accounts whisky was his staple diet, and inviting people to try and hit him was his one way of obtaining the wherewithal to purchase his daily sustenance.

But I have not only read that nobody ever succeeded in

57

knocking him off his handkerchief, which is ridiculous if you give the matter a second's serious thought, but that nobody ever really caught him with a solid punch during his days in the ring. This is just as ridiculous. One glance at any of the few photographs in existence of Young Griffo will show that he sported a pair of cauliflower ears of remarkable shape and beauty. He was, in fact, marked far more than any of the above-named champions he fought. Most surprising for a man reputed to be so fast that he could simply reach out into the air and catch flies on the wing!

The true facts are probably that Griffo developed his amazing slipperiness the hard way: by trial and error. A tradition has grown up in boxing that the scientific and defensive boxer avoids all the clouts and that the rugged and aggressive type is wide open to them. I don't believe this to be so, even generally speaking. A light-hitting pugilist who is obliged to box his way to a points decision over ten, fifteen, or even twenty rounds naturally indulges in far more exchanges than the heavier hitter with a poor defence who finishes his fights, or has them finished for him, inside the distance.

Jim Driscoll, who is acknowledged as having been one of the cleverest boxers of all time, could never have been mistaken by anyone who met him for what he was. His trade was written indelibly on his face. The same may be said of Johnny Basham, another Fancy Dan. On the other hand, Stanley Ketchel, whose inclination was always to plunge in to close quarters with both fists hooking and swinging, regardless of defence, was unmarked by comparison. Jack Doyle, who was usually a wild clouter from first to last, didn't have a blemish on him.

There *are* exceptions, of course. There always are. Among the clever men, Jim Corbett, Gene Tunney and Billy Wells, for instance, bore little or no evidence on their faces that they were prizefighters. Among the more rugged gentry, Tom Sharkey, Jim Jeffries and Bob Fitzsimmons could state their profession without saying a word.

8 A Nightmare Fight

The protagonists were James J. Jeffries, heavyweight champion of the world, and Tom Sharkey, the fighting sailor from San Francisco. The battle they waged for the title ranks as one of the hardest contests two pugilists ever fought. It is doubtful if any other men than Jeffries and Sharkey, the toughest of the tough, could have stood up under the frightful conditions of this famous meeting. It went the full distance of twenty-five rounds, with Jeffries being returned the winner on points, yet never at any time was he the complete master of the situation. For many years afterwards a considerable percentage of the sporting public claimed that Sharkey should have been awarded a draw, at least. For a very long period Sharkey himself appeared to subscribe to this opinion, and it was only when he finally admitted that Jeffries had been the better man that night – an admission he made to the old champion personally when both were elderly men – that some part of the public ceased insisting that Sharkey had been robbed.

James J. Jeffries was one of the mightiest of all the legendary champions. He was built more like a wrestler than a boxer : solid and thick clean through. From all accounts he had no particular natural aptitude or liking for the sport in which he chose to make a living. Tommy Ryan, the middleweight champion, is the man credited with developing him into the formidable fighter he eventually became. While sparring with the big youngster, Ryan noticed in him a tendency to fall into a sort of crouch while under attack, which made him hard to reach. Ryan encouraged it, and it was this unorthodox stance, coupled with a ponderous but extremely powerful straight, left-handed smash of a punch which he delivered coming up out of that crouch, which laid the basis of his success and fortune. He was tremendously strong, had enormous stamina, and appeared almost impervious to punishment. He was also unimaginative : a good quality in his type of pugilist. For many years connoisseurs of the sport reckoned him as possibly the greatest fighter of all time in a hypothetical fight to a finish between the best. In more recent years only the durable Rocky Marciano has been thought to be his equal.

Tom Sharkey was a fighter cast in much the same mould, although not so big. He had no pretensions to style or boxing artistry, but went in punching with both fists and taking whatever came his way. Built like the squat schooner he had tattooed across his chest, it took the very best of storms to sink him. He had had an up-and-down career but, if anything, he was a more unimaginative man that Jim Jeffries. Defeats meant nothing to him : he still believed he was the best. Admittedly none too bright, his stolid mentality attracted certain exaggerations. At one time he kept a saloon with the old-fashioned swinging doors. Wilson Mizner said of him : 'He was so dumb that he crawled under them for two years before he found out that they swung both ways.'

This battle between Jeffries and Sharkey took place on the evening of 3 November, 1899, at the Coney Island Athletic Club, New York, and the motion picture people were responsible for the terrible conditions under which it was fought. Earlier sporting events had been filmed under artifical lights but had produced no successful moving pictures, and on this occasion it had been decided that powerful lamps, extremely bright and consequently very hot, should be suspended above the ring. In order to obtain their maximum benefit they were hung literally only a few feet over the heads of the contestants. With some understandable exaggeration, Jeffries stated that the lights were strong enough to illuminate a city of forty thousand, and that they were so low that he could reach up and touch them with his gloves. He probably thought he could, but the photographs of the fight prove that although the lamps were ridiculously low they were not quite so low as all that.

But their heat was overpowering. Many ringside reporters and spectators fainted from the temperature, and the heat could be felt as far back as the twelfth row. How Jeffries and Sharkey fought their great battle right beneath these lights, stripped to the waist, is something of a mystery. The champion described the conditions as follows :

... It was like standing at the mouth of a blast furnace, and hotter than the blast from a locomotive when the fire door is opened.

Within a minute after climbing into the ring the water was pouring off my body, soaking my tights and running into my eyes, and all the time the great heat was drying it on to me, so that we were being parboiled and baked at the same time.

The heat was harder on me than it was on Sharkey. I was more than a foot taller, and my head was that much closer to the lamps, so that, at times, in the fight, the hair seemed to be scorching.*

If Jeffries was a foot the taller man, that made his challenger about five feet one-and-half : a statement which is ridiculous. Actually, Sharkey stood about five feet eight or nine, while the bigger Jeffries, who fought almost throughout in his famous crouch, was often farther from the lights than his opponent. Both men were probably equally inconvenienced, and George Siler, who refereed the fight and spent a considerable part of it in trying to tear the two men apart when they clinched, experienced as uncomfortable a time as either. Throughout the whole twenty-five rounds, however, he wore a wide-brimmed hat.

Tom Sharkey had trained thoroughly for this contest, for he dearly wanted to win the championship, and from the opening bell he carried the fight to his taller and heavier adversary with the object of knocking out Jeffries with one of his pile-driving punches. He stayed on the offensive throughout the encounter, and while he failed to put Jeffries down for the count he did manage to give the big fellow an uncomfortable time, and although the sailor took the best of the champion's terrible punches he absorbed everything that came his way and he was fighting strongly until the final bell. You had to knock him cold before he would even consider the possibility that he had been licked. Even then he was inclined to put up an argument.

We have it on very good authority that Jeffries injured his left elbow in training and that at no time during the fight was he able to use that arm with its best effect. If, as Jeffries himself insisted, he actually fought with a broken bone in that elbow,

* Hugh Fullerton. *Two Fisted Jeff* (Consolidated Book Publishers, Chicago, 1929).

the pain that it must undoubtedly have caused him, together with the extreme discomfort from the lights, indicate courage and grit of the highest order.

Tom Sharkey fared no better – considerably worse, in fact – for he most certainly sustained three broken ribs in the seventeenth round, and one of them stuck out through the skin for the remainder of the bout. If such an injury were caused in these more squeamish days the fight would be stopped there and then, even if the fighter did not retire from the fray immediately. But in 1899 Tom Sharkey gave no thought at all to giving in and the referee made no attempt to halt proceedings.

There is little doubt that Jeffries had slightly the better of the milling, despite Sharkey's permanent aggressiveness. For instance, the champion scored all the knock-downs that were in evidence. He put the sailor flat on to his back in the second round with a tremendous blow, and probably any other man but the hard-as-nails challenger would never have climbed erect after taking a punch like that one. But Sharkey not only bounced back, he tore into Jeffries like a demon, and all the champion's efforts to finish him off at that moment were frustrated.

Sharkey was dropped to the canvas on several other occasions during the battle, usually from powerful swipes to the side of the head, but each time he came back full of fight. Jeffries was trying his hardest to land cleanly on the jaw, but the challenger kept his chin well protected with his shoulder and those mighty lunges from his opponent invariably connected in the region of Sharkey's left ear. Towards the end of the bitter struggle that ear swelled up under the bombardment and then burst. The champion has said that whenever he landed on it it was like hitting a big wet sponge. He had also split Sharkey's eyebrow, so there was plenty of blood in evidence – mostly the sailor's – but Jeffries did not escape completely. His own brow was cut late in the fight, and although this did little to inconvenience him, it counts in Sharkey's favour, despite the champion's insistence that the cut was caused by a head-on collision, so to speak, of the two craniums.

To those spectators well away from the ring, Sharkey appeared to be getting all the better of the encounter. He never stopped attacking and swinging, but those close to the ringside, and the referee in particular, saw that Jeffries' ponderous straight-lefts and right-hand smashes to the head were scoring more often than the smaller man's wild but spirited swings. Sharkey flopped on to his stool at the end of each round in a state of apparent exhaustion, but he always came out for the following round with a determined rush and charged into his opponent. Probably no fighter in history ever tried harder to win a fight than Sharkey did this one. He seemed made of iron, he was tremendously strong and game, and in excellent physical condition. Not once did he let up in his attack, and this aggressiveness was the cause of one very unusual incident.

Jeffries always said that it happened in the twenty-third round, but all other contemporary authorities are unanimous in agreeing that it occurred in the last round : actually only a few moments before the bell. Rather surprisingly, it is seldom ever mentioned in accounts of the fight, and you will have to dig deep into pugilistic archives to find anything about it. The men were breaking from a clinch, and Jeffries, in an effort to wrench his left arm free, tore it loose but left his glove under Sharkey's arm. George Siler immediately waved the sailor back and intervened in order to readjust the glove. But all Sharkey could see was Jeffries, and he dodged round the referee and aimed a punch at the champion. Now Jeffries' left wrist was being held by the referee as he prepared to fix on the glove, and his right fist was on the other side of Siler. Defending himself instinctively, Jeffries yanked his left away from the referee and the loose glove and struck out at Sharkey in an effort to keep him away. He hit his opponent with a bare fist : an illegal blow under Queensberry rules, but an incident that could well be overlooked under the circumstances. Sharkey was fighting mad and knew only one thing : to keep at Jeffries and pound at him until the fight was over. The bell was almost due, and Sharkey was staging the pugilistic equivalent of a final spurt. It is doubtful if he realised at the time that he was being hit with the raw 'un. He certainly showed no signs of feeling it any more than the gloved punches.

The last two rounds of this amazing fight were like a nightmare. Neither man had proved to be overwhelmingly the better, but each felt that he had a slight advantage over the other, and both fought all the harder to clinch matters. Several times during those last hectic six minutes Jeffries had Sharkey in a bad way, but each time the challenger shook off the effects of the punches and came back as fiercely as ever. Sweat rolled off them like water as they smashed blindly at each other, and when the bell sounded for the end of the fight they were still pounding away like madmen.

As they dropped their arms and stood gasping, George Siler immediately raised Jeffries' arm in the accustomed token of victory, and a great roar went up. Half of the spectators were cheering the decision and the other half were loudly expressing their disapproval of the verdict. Tom Sharkey, who was disappointed and terribly mauled, but – unbelievably – still full of fight, demanded another chance right away. He then retired to his corner and sat dispiritedly on his stool as his seconds removed his gloves. He had put up the finest performance in his entire career.

Those who saw Sharkey fight agreed that he was never quite the same man again. Jeffries and the heat took a tremendous amount from him that night. He went to hospital the moment he left the arena and he stopped there for three days. The champion was in better condition than his opponent but had fared pretty badly all the same. Read what Jeffries had to say at the close of his own description of that struggle :

> I lost close to twenty pounds during the battle. The canvas of the ring was soaked with blood and sweat until we waded in water that oozed up when we stepped around.
>
> To show what we underwent in that struggle, both Tom and I had fine heads of hair when we went into the ring. Within a week our hair started to fall out and we became nearly bald, and today, as far as the hair crop is concerned, Tom and I get a draw. Maybe I have a shade of three hairs on him, but not more.*

Here, as in much of what he had to say, further embellished by a highly-imaginative ghost-writer, there is considerable exaggeration. But both fighters certainly were premature baldies. They did *not*, however, become 'nearly bald' within the matter of a few weeks, as Jeffries suggests. Photographs of his very last fight – that versus Jack Johnson more than ten years later

* *Two Fisted Jeff.*

– show him to be thinning on top, but still fairly well covered. Sharkey, who was introduced from the ring before that same contest, and who was photographed too, also retained much of his hair.

At the start of the famous Jeffries-Sharkey fight, the champion weighed about fifteen stone four pounds. Sharkey's weight was in the region of thirteen stone. The purse was $25,000 and the gate receipts totalled $68,000. Ringside seats were priced at $35 each, and so popular was this impending battle that these dearer seats were the first to sell out. Jeffries was favoured at 10–7 in the betting to retain his title, and there is no doubt that he did so despite the outcry that a draw would have been the fairest decision. That Jeffries was out and about the following morning while Sharkey was admitted to hospital 'more dead than alive', as one writer put it, is proof enough that the sailor did not have the better of things. In fact, Inspector McLaughlin, of the New York police, ordered the champion not to leave the city until Sharkey was out of danger.

The films of the Jeffries-Sharkey fight were successfully shot, but only at great cost to the two men who put up this thrilling and arduous battle for supremacy. There is an interesting sequel rarely told concerning those motion pictures, which, like most of the fight films of that era, had a little phoney business about them.

It seems that the company which made the pictures had not registered them at the Patents Office, and a rival firm was not long in pirating the film and issuing what was termed a 'bootleg version' of the encounter. It was rather belatedly decided that if one round – the last, perhaps – could be re-fought and re-shot by the cameras, with the action differing, as was inevitable, from the original film, then the whole thing could be copyrighted and the rival concern outwitted. Jeffries was in condition to waltz through another three minutes under the lights, but Sharkey was still at home recuperating in bed. He was actually induced to get up, don ring togs, and go through a staged last round again. 'Extras' were recruited from the Coney Island streets to act as the ringside spectators and reporters, but George Siler, the referee, was not available. He was impersonated by William Brady, Jeffries' manager, who put on a battered old hat of the same kind Siler had worn throughout

c   65

the affair on 3 November. Nowadays, of course, with cinematography so far advanced that every feature of the men in the ring is clearly recorded on celluloid, such a deception would be impossible. In 1899 it worked like a charm, and very few people who saw those films at the time were aware that the last hectic session was not *bona fide,* or that the man who raised Jeffries' arm at the close of the contest was not the perspiring Siler who had been struggling in the clinches and been dodging Sharkey's wild swipes for twenty-five rounds.

Not surprisingly, Tom Sharkey's career, which had shown him on the up-grade until this point, now took a perceptible turn for the worse. The following year, when he returned to activity, he did manage to score a few impressive victories over none-too-formidable opposition, but then he was surprisingly beaten by Gus Ruhlin, a man whom he had knocked out in less than a round almost exactly two years earlier. Then old Bob Fitzsimmons summarily disposed of him in two, something the mighty Jeffries had been unable to accomplish in twenty-five. Both of these fights, incidentally, also took place at Coney Island, a venue which did not exactly prove a fortunate one for Tom Sharkey. The fighting sailor's rumbustious days within the ropes virtually came to an end in 1902, when Ruhlin knocked him out in the eleventh round in London. That Gus Ruhlin himself, in his own attempt to wrest the championship from Jeffries, had put up an inglorious display and had been unable to answer the bell for the fifth round, gives some sort of indication of how Sharkey had deteriorated. He was not yet thirty when he elected to earn his daily bread by less strenuous means. The wonder to me is that he ever climbed into a ring again, or even wished to, after that nightmare fight with Jim Jeffries.

9 Ring Oddities – I

Towards the end of 1968 the British flyweight champion, John McCluskey, signed to box an up-and-coming young bantam-weight named Johnny Clark. Shortly before their contest it was discovered that whereas one of the protagonists had signed on the understanding that they were to meet over ten rounds, the other had agreed to the match being of only eight rounds.

There is no doubt that both camps held an honest opinion about the matter: each boxer had trained to go the number of rounds for which he genuinely believed this contest had been stipulated. Now, while to the uninitiated observer there may appear very little difference between eight rounds of boxing and ten, there is a *great* deal of difference to the particular athlete who is obliged to do the boxing.

In this particular instance, neither side was prepared to capitulate: one said eight, the other said ten. At first, it was a deadlock, and it looked like the fight was off. But eventually common sense prevailed. Both sides agreed on a compromise. How's about a bout over nine?

McCluskey and Clark eventually boxed a very fine contest over this agreed, if unusual distance. It received quite a lot of publicity. Harry Carpenter, that extremely knowledgeable and enthusiastic television sports commentator, while reporting this fight on B.B.C.'s *Grandstand*, mentioned that he knew of no other contracted nine-round contest. But there *was* one, before the war, and when I gave Harry Carpenter the full details he informed me that he wished he had had this information at the time of the McCluskey-Clark fight. It is certainly a boxing oddity, and would have been well worth reporting during his commentary.

Back in the nineteen-thirties, one of the busiest professionals in this country was a Battersea middleweight-cum-cruiser named Frank Hough. He was a good 'un, but a little short of the championship calibre of contemporaries like Jock McAvoy and Len Harvey. He started off the year 1938 by announcing that he would box a ten-rounder *every week*. The records will show that he appeared at the old Empress Hall on 10, 17, 24 January, and 7 and 14 February on the regular Earl's Court Monday night show. Not content with that programme, he had also signed to box a ten-rounder versus Marcel Bazin at Marylebone for 17 February.

Unfortunately, one of the British Boxing Board of Control's rules was that no man should box two ten-round bouts within seven days. The Bazin contest was therefore billed as a nine-round meeting, and a further perusal of the records will reveal that Hough outpointed Marcel Bazin over that odd distance.

As a point of interest, Frank Hough went on to box three more ten-round bouts on 3, 10 and 21 March. But Tommy Martin knocked him out in the last one, and Hough wisely abandoned his intensive campaign until the summer.

10   One-Round Knock-outs — and a Reminiscence

The public's capacity for self-deception would appear to be illimitable. One has only to look at professional wrestling, popularised by television, to see this. For week after week and for month after month wrestling exhibitions follow the same pattern – with minor variations. Wrestler A gains the first fall, wrestler B equalises, and then comes the final and decisive fall. These 'best two out of three' engagements are invariably extended to between six and eight rounds. Occasionally, when an exhibition is advertised as being a single-fall match, the bout surprisingly stretches for roughly the same length of time.

Few addicts seem to question this sort of coincidence seriously. The wrestlers are so obviously and so undeniably hurting each other that the average spectator convinces himself that the whole thing *must* be on the level. It rarely occurs to him that stunt men in the films he sees are genuinely getting hurt, too, and occasionally getting killed if things go wrong, but that the action still follows the story line. The hero, or rather the stunt-man doubling for the hero in long-shot, invariably over-comes the villain, or the villain's double, anyway.

I never cease to be amazed at the sameness and monotony of the choreography in the wrestling matches. I have been watching the entertainment, purely *as* entertainment, I hasten to add, on and off for more than thirty-five years. Basically, the pattern of the thing has been much the same during the whole time. I have now attained a proficiency of anticipation where I can say, confidently, but somewhat hurriedly: 'Pin fall coming up in the next two or three seconds.' I don't doubt that others more well-versed than I can better this.

In my youth, when I first attended wrestling, and when television was little more than a pipe-dream, I was quite con-vinced that the whole thing was *bona fide*. But I attended association football, too, and nothing could have convinced me then that each soccer player wasn't doing his level best. Rather more recent disclosures have shown that not *all* football heroes were honest. As far as I am concerned, these disclosures did not prove that some players of the Fifties and Sixties were corrupt, but only that some former stars of the soccer field didn't get found out.

Now, in boxing you get the one-round knock-out. Some-times this is caused by a fortuitous blow by one man before the other has really warmed up. Just as often it happens be-cause one pugilist is far superior to his opponent. Similar things sometimes occur in soccer when an outstanding first-division team gets drawn against a non-league side in a third-round cup-tie. You get something approaching a cricket score: foot-ball's necessarily ninety-minute equivalent of boxing's one-round knock-out. But it almost never happens in professional wrestling. In fact, looking back at well over a quarter of a century's participation in wrestling – audience participation, of course – I can recall only one bout which endured for a matter of seconds rather than of minutes.

This took place one rainy Sunday afternoon many, many years ago in a water-logged ring set up in the middle of a dog-track in North London. The main bout of the extravaganza was an exciting battle between a redoubtable Champion and a colourful Foreign Menace. This was only the second or third tournament I had ever witnessed : I was still impressed by the drama and uncertainty of the whole thing, and I was enthralled. What I did not know, but learned later, was that the two protagonists were related by marriage, could almost be termed blood-brothers, and had gone through all this hoo-hah many times before. (I saw them go through it many times again, in later months.)

The script demanded that Champion should win, after a most heroic struggle. I never witnessed any deviation, except on this one occasion. This time the referee apparently decided, without consulting those most intimately concerned, to write in a new ending. He disqualified Champion at the very height of the excitement. Champion, whose vanity was pricked, to say the very least, forthwith knocked senseless both his opponent *and* the referee.

Champion stalked from the ring in high dudgeon, to the shouts and boos of a lynch-crazy audience. Only the fact that there was still another bout to come deterred the frenzied crowd from mobbing him.

This last contest was billed to feature a certain journeyman Jumbo from Holland, whose opponent had not turned up. The aforementioned redoubtable Champion, in order to placate a disgruntled crowd and to restore to its proper shape his deflated ego, elected to come back, still hot, tired and sweaty from his earlier encounter, to do battle with this fresh Foreign Menace.

The first round lasted a few seconds. Champion clamped Jumbo in an excruciating head-scissors and was awarded the first fall by a submission in less time than it takes me to type it. (The referee who awarded it, by the way, was also a substitute.)

Round two followed almost precisely the same pattern. Ten seconds : another head-scissors, and another submission. Champion won by two straight falls, in the shortest wrestling match I have ever seen. He swelled his chest, looked disdainfully at a jeering mob, and made his exit.

Now I am not unaware that this whole thing might more than probably have been pre-arranged. But it was all done so well that after all these years I still have nagging doubts. I relate it simply because it marks the only occasion on which I have witnessed a professional wrestling match which was over inside one minute, with breathing space between rounds included.

Other lightning victories *have* occurred in the past, I know. (Students of the history of wrestling, please don't quote me Georges Hackenschmidt. I used to work for him before the war, heard him talk, and know quite a bit about his career. I also know what Gama did to Zbyscko, too, in India. But those fellows were *really* wrestling.)

But this is supposed to be a book about boxing, says you. Why drag in wrestling? Only as a comparison, gentle reader, nothing more. Don't you consider them allied sports? Bear with me a little longer.

I have done my best to show how rarely lightning victories occur in modern wrestling. This, I submit, is because the promoters are intent upon giving their customers plenty of entertainment and full value for money. They long ago learned that wrestling matches waged entirely upon the respective merits of the two opponents will either result in completely one-sided farces or in dour, dull struggles which can literally last for hours without either man putting much more than his knee to the mat.

I have had something to do with amateur wrestling, which, by its very definition, is ninety-nine and nine-tenths per cent straight. If you are close enough to the contestants – that is, if you know them personally, and are within about six feet's proximity to them, the whole thing can be absorbing. But as a spectator sport, pure and simple, it doesn't even attract flies. I can recall the occasion of two snails copulating on the stem of a plant which I swear drew a far more rapt group of onlookers than any amateur wrestling match that I can remember.

The more evenly-matched the two wrestlers are, the more boring the struggle they will exhibit if their contest is an honest one. This does not apply to boxers, who ought rarely to come to grips. Admittedly, boxing *can* be terribly dull, particularly to those who don't know a lot about it. Mr and Mrs Everyman will sit and watch the televised film of a fifteen-round championship fight because there had been a big build-up about it for weeks, and because the morning paper had told them the bout was a classic. They will often wonder what the fuss was about. No knock-downs, no knock-out, and very few thrills.

They will tell each other that neither boxer could last a minute with Matt Dillon in a knuckle-fight in the dust outside the main street saloon, and they will switch over to late-night wrestling. The true fight fan is different. He knew what it was all about, and he followed every move. And, when all is said and done, there is no denying that a much larger public will watch a television boxing match rather than a wrestling match, and a great many more people will pay to see an actual boxing contest in preference to a wrestling exhibition, if there is the slightest possibility that something dramatic will be on view.

The fact is that although boxing and wrestling are somehow considered to be similar sports, they are really like chalk and cheese. They both take place in the same sort of ring, they are bouts of unarmed single combat, and the contestants usually strip to shorts. There the resemblance ends.

The one-round knock-out in boxing, although far more frequent than the one-round termination in modern wrestling, is nevertheless a fairly rare occurrence. Very few boxers have been so good that they have been able to make a habit of winning in this fashion at all stages of their careers. Quite a number have started off in sensational style when opposed to second- and third-raters, and have then found themselves obliged to settle down a little more when facing stiffer propositions. But Dempsey was one man who specialised in brevity right up to the time he won the world's championship. Louis was another. He, of course, went on knocking men cold with a punch or two right from his mere 'prentice days until the time he was facing top-notchers in defence of his title. I particularly remember that along towards the end of his busy career, at a time when everyone was expecting to hear of his retirement, he completely demolished his leading contender, Tami Mauriello, in one of the most exciting first rounds ever seen in an American ring. Carpentier, too, frequently got things over very early. He was so fast that he often knocked his opponents out before they had properly warmed up and got into their stride.

But these men were pugilistic geniuses. People paid to see them because of the prospect of sudden and early drama. In addition, they were types who had difficulty in pulling their punches in order to extend a contest.

On the other hand, there were men like Sam Langford.

72

Operating at a time when coloured fighters were the exception rather than the rule, and underprivileged, to say the least, his record does not reflect his true ability. He frequently fought 'under wraps', so to speak. Promoters often demanded that he stretch out a contest to make some sort of show, when it was obvious to many people concerned that he was quite capable of clouting his man into oblivion with a single punch. Langford was obliged to toe the line or starve. If he were fighting today, when men of his complexion outnumber the white pugilists by far, particularly in the United States, it is my opinion that he would have been scoring many, many one-round knockouts and would be a very rich man, as well as a champion.

11   Apocryphal – II

In the early nineteen-twenties, Benny Leonard, the brilliant lightweight champion, was so superior to all other men of his weight that he elected to step out of his division and face the equally brilliant welterweight champion, Jack Britton. The outcome of this fight formed the basis of that remarkable short story by Ernest Hemingway, *Fifty Grand*.

In 1950, Lillian Ross wrote one of the famous *New Yorker* 'Profiles', and her subject was the aforementioned Hemingway. During her piece she quoted him quite a lot. Here I quote *her* quoting him :

Jack Britton, he continued, was a fighter he admired very much . . . He straightened up and looked thoughtfully at his glass. Then he said, 'One time, I asked Jack, speaking of a fight with Benny Leonard, "How did you handle Benny so easy, Jack?" "Ernie," he said, "Benny is an awfully smart boxer. All the time he's boxing, he's thinking. All the time he was thinking, I was hitting him." ' Hemingway gave a hoarse laugh, as though he had heard the story for the first time. 'Jack moved very geometrically pure, never one hundredth of an inch too much. No one ever got a solid shot at him. Wasn't anybody he couldn't hit any time he wanted to.' He laughed again. ' "All the time he was thinking, I was hitting him." ' The anecdote, he told me, had been in the original version of *Fifty Grand,* but Scott Fitzgerald had persuaded him to take it out. 'Scott thought everybody knew about it, when only Jack Britton and I knew about it, because Jack told it to me,' he said.*

I am not surprised that Fitzgerald induced Hemingway to delete that yarn. Back in 1911, Sam Langford beat Bill Lang rather easily in London. Soon afterwards, Eugene Corri, the famous referee, mentioned to the winner that his opponent had the reputation for fighting with his brains. Langford's reply to this, made before the First World War, and published by Corri shortly after the war, was as follows : 'He's pretty fast on his feet, but his brains ain't fast. While he was thinking, I was hitting him !'

I doubt if either Hemingway or Jack Britton ever read Corri's memoirs. I don't think they needed to. That tale was common gossip in gymnasiums long before either put on a boxing glove or wrote a story. Corri heard it first from Langford, and probably thought it was original. Langford, in turn, might well have had it told to him years earlier. I'm glad Scott Fitzgerald persuaded Hemingway to cut it out of *Fifty Grand.*

12   The Irish Nightingale

Anyone who spends very much time in the vicinity of that widely-publicised and diversely-populated region of London known as Notting Hill Gate cannot avoid, sooner or later, either passing or meeting a certain imposing-looking man of middle-age. He stands six feet four, and he is very erect. The

* Lillian Ross. *Portrait of Hemingway* (Penguin, 1962).

last time I saw him his hair was still as black and as curly as it always had been. There was a little more flesh about his jowls than there used to be, and I don't doubt that there was considerably more round his waist than in the old days. But from the well-cut suit he was wearing you'd never guess it.

Women are inclined to give him the old double-take when they pass him. He's that sort of chap. Men of his own age tend to envy him his size and appearance, and to wonder if he's a 'somebody'. They seem to think that they have seen that face before. They have. Perhaps they saw it in photographs of the gossip columns. Probably they saw it in the pictures on the sports pages. More probably they saw it on the screen, on the stage, or – fleetingly – in the ring. He's that broth of a bhoy, Jack Doyle.

Ireland has produced some flamboyant characters, wholly and partly. Brendan Behan, Errol Flynn and John L. Sullivan were three. Jack Doyle had a little of each of them in him. He couldn't write like Behan, but he had the same sort of capacity for roistering and for keeping things in an uproar. Perhaps he didn't have the same polish of Flynn as an actor, but I think the girls loved him just as much. In the ring he certainly wasn't as consistently successful as Sullivan, but I am inclined to think that of the two he probably carried the harder punch. Oh, and by the way, he had a touch of the John McCormacks about him, too. Jack Doyle could also sing.

I first heard of him back in 1932. He was then about eighteen, and the *Daily Mail*'s boxing writer, Geoffrey Simpson, couldn't seem to write enough about him. Doyle was then a fledgeling soldier in the Irish Guards, and what he was doing to the other young guardsmen in the boxing tournaments was really out of this world. Within a very short space of time Doyle was bought out of the army, placed under the protective wing of that canny old schemer, Dan Sullivan, and was launched on the most colourful career of any fighter I can think of this side of the Atlantic.

Had he never joined the army as a youth and been induced to put on the gloves, it is just possible that Jack Doyle might

75

never have been heard of outside of County Cork. But I doubt it. One way or another, I think he would have been pushed into the limelight. As it happened, professional pugilism claimed him.

I use the word pugilism here advisedly. The word boxing carries certain connotations. Very broadly speaking, I suppose, Doyle *was* a boxer, yet he would be the last man to claim any great artistic talents in this direction, using the strictest and narrowest sense of the term. He was a great big fellow with a terrific power in a bludgeoning right-hander. When he hit 'em, they usually stayed hit. Jack Doyle wasn't particularly interested much further.

His first year of campaigning was fantastic. It happened at a time when heavyweight boxing was just emerging from a period in the doldrums. The one British fighter among the big fellows who had any pretensions to an international reputation, and who had more than remotely looked like a world champion, Phil Scott, was now retired. The fighter who took his place was a midlander named Reggie Meen. This gentleman was willing enough, and he was certainly a hard trier. Unfortunately, he lost almost as many contests as he won, more often than not to foreign opposition. When, by process of elimination, he became the new British champion, nobody grew very excited. But at the same time the game was receiving a wonderful transfusion of new blood. All this seemed to occur in the wake of one Primo Carnera, a cumbersome Italian freak who had arrived in England with a fanfare of ballyhoo which proclaimed him to be so big that he was unbeatable and indestructible. It did not take long to expose this particular piece of publicity, but Carnera did, at least, pack 'em in. Fans flocked in their thousands to see him. And almost overnight, it seemed, every go-ahead British manager started looking for a great big young fellow who was capable of putting his fists up, so that he could get into the act, too.

Of these big boys, there is no doubt that Jack Doyle was the one most possessed of natural ability and colour. I stress the point about natural ability. There was nothing fancy or schooled about him : the bell rang, he charged, and he started throwing right-hand punches. His first seven fights lasted a total of nine rounds, five of them terminating in the opening round and two extending to the second. In addition, he was good-looking – and Oirish.

Of the few other serious competitors he had at this time in his rapid climb to the top was a young man named Jack Pettifer, who was, if anything, even bigger than Carnera. He may not have been so heavy as the Italian, but he was certainly as tall, or taller. His fortunes were primarily based on this fact. To his financial detriment, however, he was a big-built *boxer*. Jack Doyle was a big-built *basher*. As this pair of young giants rose swiftly in their chosen profession it became increasingly obvious that they must very soon meet.

Ironically, both of these fellows were playing second fiddle, at the time, to yet another young phenomenon. This was a Cardiff-born stripling who had had a brilliant career as an amateur, and who now, as a professional, was beginning to look like a potential world-beater. Jack Petersen, still able to weigh in at the light-heavyweight limit of twelve stone seven pounds, was going through our cruisers and heavies like the oft-mentioned dose of salts.

Doyle, in fact, was 'underneath' Petersen on the same bill several times in the Welshman's early career. The bigger young-ster overshadowed the principal each time with sensational wins, and I remember particularly that he clouted Bill Partridge into submission in the opening round on the night that Jack Petersen outpointed Harry Crossley for the British cruiser-weight title at the old Holborn Stadium, and less than a couple of months later stopped Guardsman Gater in two at Wimbledon just before Petersen took the heavyweight championship from Reggie Meen in the same brief space of time.

Later that same year, 1932, at the old Crystal Palace, a packed hall of exuberant fans practically went mad when Doyle faced up to the enormous Jack Pettifer. It was action from start to finish in their short but hectic clash. At the opening bell Doyle charged and started throwing rights. Pettifer met him in the centre of the ring and stopped him short with long straight-lefts to the face. Again and again the Irishman made his rush, and again and again the Londoner pulled him up short with that classic ramrod left. It was like fighting bull and matador as the maddened and frustrated Doyle shook off those punches and hurled himself forward in a renewed attack. But

77

no bull ever took so much punishment as Jack Doyle received in those opening few minutes. When the bell ended the first round he was still fighting crazy, his face was reddened by the cumulative effect of Pettifer's punches, and he had hardly scored an effective blow himself.

The second round opened to exactly the same pattern. Doyle charged, took everything, but still came on. Then, about halfway through the round, and to the accompaniment of the shrieks from a delirious audience, he rushed blindly into the attack and for the first time in the fight he beat Pettifer to the punch. His right caught the big fellow perfectly on the point of the jaw. Big Jack went down with a bang on to his back, his head and shoulders hanging over the bottom rope. It was the perfect knock-out : he could not have got to his feet had the referee counted a hundred. Doyle stood in the centre of the ring like a bull waiting for somebody else to come out and continue the fight. He looked disappointed that the whole thing was over. I believe he would have loved it had Pettifer been able to get up and carry on.

This remarkable win earned Jack Doyle a chance at Petersen's British title and Lonsdale Belt. After a couple more dramatic successes against inferior opposition he signed to meet the champion in an open-air show at the White City in July, 1933, after only ten professional contests. This fight was the first of the several disappointments Jack Doyle taught us all to expect when he was on view.

Just why he acted in the way he did that evening has never been satisfactorily explained. Some of the commentators said that the occasion was too much for one so young and inexperienced. Whatever the explanation, he seemed to fight with an almost total disregard for the rules. Petersen himself was something of a two-fisted attacker ever ready to have a go, and he met Doyle in the centre of the ring with both gloves swinging. But the Irishman, who had hitherto favoured a wild attack to the head and jaw, now started throwing punches to the body. Some were on the borderline and many were palpably low. In vain the referee called to him to keep his punches up, but again and again he landed weakening blows which were well below the belt.

He was given a great deal of latitude : the referee was reluctant to stop a fight in which so much was at stake. But by the end of the first round Petersen was in pretty bad physical shape, although he was incensed by the continual low punches and had no thought of taking the easy way out. Half the crowd was shrieking for Doyle's disqualification and the other half was yelling for Petersen to fight back in kind. The referee followed Doyle to his corner and warned him quite clearly that he had given him his last chance.

But Jack Doyle appeared to be past all understanding. The second round was only a few moments old before his punches were again going well below the belt. The referee immediately stopped the fiasco and sent Doyle to his corner. For the first time in his career he was booed from the ring.

Doyle's share of the purse was something over £3,000. This, of course, was automatically confiscated, pending an enquiry. The Board of Control claimed that Doyle was not entitled to the money, and a long legal wrangle ensured. I believe the Irishman eventually won his case, and received the money he claimed was due to him, but it kept him out of the ring for many months. He also grew very disillusioned with professional boxing as an occupation, and I think we can safely say that it was at about this point that he ceased to be looked upon as an up-and-coming young heavyweight and potential champion. His career was to continue for several years, but although nobody was to know it, he had already fought about half the contests in which he was ever to engage.

From this moment forward, Jack Doyle's name was hardly ever out of the newspapers for more than a few weeks. He was the reporters' dream, as far as copy is concerned. I recall his taking to the music-hall stage, for instance, as a singer. He was a fair tenor, without having any pretensions to grand opera or the concert hall. In some places he was received very well, but in others, unfortunately, the reverse was true. On one occasion, before his own countrymen, if memory serves me right, he was pelted from the gallery with rotten fruit and vegetables. It was a case of Doyle being more sinned against than sinning. When I think of some of the more recent pop stars who have earned thousands a week and mass adulation for their cater-wauling, I am inclined towards the opinion that Jack Doyle received a very raw deal in this direction.

The British film industry saw him as a potential rival to Errol Flynn in swashbuckling movies. He made only one picture of any importance : *McGluskey the Sea Rover,* based on one of those popular adventure tales by A. G. Hales. It would be difficult to imagine a worse piece of miscasting : the original McGluskey of the stories was an ugly, broken-nosed adventurer and soldier of fortune who might have been played by someone like Victor McLaglen or Harry Andrews, and Doyle was a good-looking matinée idol type. Be that as it may, the film had a fair success, and Doyle turned in a passable enough perform-ance. But it was evident to the producers that he wasn't going to develop into a new Douglas Fairbanks. His celluloid career lapsed.

Jack Doyle fought in the ring only once in 1934. They put him in against a tough heavyweight named Frank Borrington in a scheduled twelve-rounder at the Albert Hall in what was called his 'comeback'. The big Irishman proved that he still had the old magic of packing a hall and providing thrills. He knocked out Borrington in the opening round.

The following year he attempted an American invasion with his fists. He began well : one Phil Donato succumbed to Doyle's terrible right almost as soon as the fight started, and a few weeks later Jack Redmond earned a dubious glory by extend-ing the invader to the fourth round. This was the longest excursion within the ropes Doyle had ever enjoyed, up to this point.

Then came a disastrous affair. Max Baer, that enigmatic heavyweight who had held the world's championship for a short twelve months, had long been telling the world about his kid brother, Buddy. This youth, standing six feet six inches and scaling over seventeen stone, had been introduced into the pro-fession with much flourishing of trumpets. Max insisted that Buddy was greater than *he* was, and there was no denying that the youngster's first year in the ring was sensational. He had a string of one- and two-round knock-out triumphs behind him extending to about twenty contests, with only one defeat on points to besmirch his record.

They packed Madison Square Garden, of course. Big punchers will always provide a sell-out. But their encounter was brief, sensational and controversial. They came together like two wild bulls, and they had the onlookers off their seats in a matter of seconds. But the fight was stopped in the opening minutes, in favour of Buddy Baer, and with Jack Doyle incapacitated and on the canvas, claiming a low blow.

Doyle got a very bad press. It must be remembered that he was the first heavyweight of any importance from these isles to test his fortunes in the United States since Phil Scott, back in the late Twenties and early Thirties. Now Scott had made something of a name for himself, and for British heavyweights in general, by claiming that he had been struck by foul punches and dropping to the boards with an agonised look on his face. The New Yorkers had dubbed him Phainting Phil and the Swooning Swan of Soho. They also remembered Billy Wells's more disappointing efforts, and the records of Joe Beckett and Frank Goddard.

Doyle was written off as just another British horizontal heavyweight, and he did no more serious boxing in the States. But if the male population tended to sneer at him as the Irish Nightingale, suggesting something unmanly in the idea of a heavyweight fighter singing tenor, he was highly popular with the female of the species during his jaunt abroad. He managed to reach Hollywood, and although he failed to crash the studios he did win the heart and hand of the beautiful Judith Allen, the young film star, who had formerly been married to Gus Sonnenberg, the heavyweight wrestling champion of the world. For a time it looked as if Jack Doyle, now settled down, had turned his back upon the ring completely. We certainly heard very little about him for some time, and he did not fight once during 1936.

But if he could now no longer be termed an active professional boxer there was no evidence that he had completely retired. As Budd Schulberg once wrote of someone else, he was now 'a business-man who went to work occasionally in bathrobe and boxing gloves when the price was right'.

1937 found him back in London, and billed to face Alf Robinson at Wembley in January. Doyle ran true to form : he had his man on the canvas and hopelessly beaten in the first round, and threw the fight away by impetuously hurling another punch at the fallen man. A month later he met the tough Dutchman, Harry Staal, who managed to

81

extend the Irishman for longer than anyone to date, before the towel came sailing in from Staal's corner to save him from further punishment.

I particularly remember Jack Doyle on a certain Gala Night at the Empire Pool, Wembley, on an occasion which was Sir Arthur Elvin's contribution to that fantastic Coronation Year of 1937. Topping the bill, Jock McAvoy, the British middle-weight champion, was challenging the current light-heavyweight title-holder, Eddie Phillips, for the latter's honours. Also on view was the tiny Filipino, Small Montana, who had just lost his world flyweight crown to Benny Lynch. He was opposing Pat Palmer, a man who would have been a champion himself had he not been the contemporary of the aforementioned Benny.

But the fight that packed Wembley on this particular evening was a pairing which brought together two of the heaviest hitters of the decade, who also happened to be two of the most colourful characters of any decade. They were Jack Doyle, himself, and the former fish-pedlar from Chicago, King Levinsky.

Levinsky, who had once been Harry Krakow, was approaching the end of his career. Much of the spring had gone out of his legs, but he still had his punch. The names of the men who had tasted it over the past ten years formed quite an impressive list: Jimmy Slattery, Tommy Loughran, Johnny Risko, Primo Carnera, Paolino Uzcudun, Max Baer, Jack Dempsey, Mickey Walker, Jack Sharkey, Maxie Rosenbloom, Don McCorkindale and Walter Neusel, among others. He had also faced Joe Louis, but that matter had been so brief an occasion that Levinsky had hardly been able to get his fists up.

At this stage in Jack Doyle's career, the handsome Irishman had only fought a couple of bouts which had gone longer than two rounds. The press and public could be forgiven for believing that this forthcoming apparent imbroglio would last no longer. In fact, the general feeling of certainty that either Doyle or Levinsky would end up flattened in double-quick time after a hectic exchange of wild right-handers led to a rather remarkable statement in the newspapers.

It was announced that a certain monied sportsman was prepared to offer Jack Doyle one pound sterling for every straight-left he succeeded in landing on King Levinsky. It was further announced that Len Harvey would be present at the ringside to count those straight-lefts.

I have never been able to ascertain whether or not this was an inspired piece of publicity dreamed up in order to heighten interest in a battle which was a 'natural' from the moment both fighters signed their names to the contract, and which was primarily responsible for selling every seat in the house weeks before the tournament took place. I never heard or read a word about it after the affair was over. But I clearly remember two things : one is that I quite failed to locate Len Harvey at the ringside with field-glasses from a distance or with the naked eye from a much closer vantage-point, and the other is that Jack Doyle waged a contest that evening utterly different from anything he had shown before and completely alien to any bout he fought afterwards.

He entered the ring, resplendently attired in his vivid emerald silk trunks and whiter-than-white robe, to the deafening screams, whistles and cat-calls which now always accompanied his appearance. The swarthy Levinsky limbered up in the opposite corner, making enormous swipes at the air.

'Poor old Jack ! Poor old Jack !' yelled the crowd, in high expectation of battle, murder and sudden death, but 'poor old Jack' showed not the slightest sign of worry.

At the opening bell, Levinsky moved in and immediately began throwing overarm right swings. Doyle replied by adopting the classic boxing stance and sticking out a hard straight-left. He plonked it accurately in the centre of Levinsky's face as the American came forward, and what is more, he continued to do so relentlessly and easily for no less than twelve rounds. Doyle won every session by a good margin. There was not a single knock-down during the whole contest, although Doyle hurled over his right every once in a while to relieve the monotony. And throughout the whole twelve rounds Levinsky never wavered in his efforts to connect with one of his roundhouse lefts or rights. The few which found a target were seldom landed on anything other than an arm or a shoulder. Doyle came out of the fight completely unmarked. Levinsky, on the other hand, left the ring with both eyes almost closed and his face ballooned with lumps and bruises. If it is a fact that Jack Doyle received his pound for every straight-left he landed that evening he must have made a small fortune. There were no jeers as he climbed down the steps of the ring this time. For that matter, there wasn't all that much applause. We in the auditorium were all much too dumbfounded to give much expression either way.

I next saw this colourful figure a little over a year later, at Harringay Arena. I shall never forget this particular evening, or anything concerned with the circumstances around it. For one thing, it was pouring in a torrential downpour outside, and almost every one of the many thousands in that vast hall was sitting uncomfortably in a drenched condition. For another, it happened to be Munich Night – and you have to be old enough to remember the year 1938 clearly to know what that means. Europe was on the brink of war, and the whole of Britain was sweating on Prime Minister Neville Chamberlain's statement to the nation on that extremely wet evening.

Harringay was pervaded throughout with a feeling of apprehension over the international situation, together with a heavy gloom which the smell of damp raincoats slowly drying out from a concerted body warmth did nothing at all to alleviate. Chamberlain's speech on the radio was relayed to the audience over the loudspeakers between bouts, but his voice was woolly and barely audible. Few people present were fully aware whether those lugubrious tones were informing us that we were going to war with Germany or not. Whatever Chamberlain actually said that night it did little to lighten our mood. That task was reserved for Jack Doyle.

The main event of that evening was the pairing of the Irish Nightingale with the cockney stylist, Eddie Phillips. This magnificently-built boxer had outgrown the light-heavyweight division and was now in the process of making quite a name for himself among the bigger fellows. I have always believed that his greatest drawback was a too highly-coloured imagination and a nervousness at the moment of a big occasion – something he shared with Billy Wells. He always reminded me of the finely-trained thoroughbred race-horse at the starting

84

gate, shying and rearing at the snap of fingers. The ideal pugilist, of course, should also have just a little of the cart-horse about him.

Eddie Phillips came into that ring as though the Prime Minister had elected him to be the first to go over the top against the Germans. It was the practice at Harringay upon the entrance of the gladiators for the main bout for all the house lights to be extinguished and for a spotlight to pick out the principals on their way to the ring, accompanied by a fanfare of trumpets. Phillips obviously didn't like the glare, and he entered the arena with head down and eyes closed, with one hand on the shoulder of a preceding second, who guided him down the aisle and through the milling mob to the ring. He looked for all the world like a man going to the gallows or the executioner's block.

Jack Doyle's entrance was in marked contrast. The moment the spotlight picked him out, the whole place erupted in its usual welcome. Say what you like about him as a boxer or a fighter, I have never known a sporting personality to compare with him in his effect upon a crowd. In a matter of seconds the atmosphere of Harringay changed completely. Nobody particularly bothered just then whether or not Britain was going to war. All that mattered for the moment was what Jack Doyle would do in the next few minutes.

I have dealt with this extraordinary contest elsewhere in these pages. It is enough to say here that we all wondered if Doyle would knock Phillips out or if Phillips would knock Doyle out. The Irishman, of course, fooled us all: he knocked himself out. Phillips got the credit for it, but the facts are that his opponent missed a terrific right-hander which was intended to be a finisher, fell out of the ring head first, and was lucky that he didn't break his neck into the bargain. Eddie Phillips had his arm raised in the usual token, but I am inclined to think that there was never a more embarrassed winner.

Well, we didn't go to war in 1938. There was that reassuring scrap of paper, and 'peace in our time'. Life went on. It is a hackneyed phrase, I know, but I am aware of no better one: there truly *was* a false sense of security.

Came the summer of 1939. The place: White City Stadium, and another big evening of boxing. Although we were not to know it at the time, this was the last great open-air tournament in London before war did break out. Top of the bill was a fifteen-rounder between Len Harvey and Jock McAvoy, styled as being for the vacant light-heavyweight championship of the world. The programme was also studded with plenty of other important names, each of which contributed towards amassing a record crowd. But I think that there was no doubt in anybody's mind that the one real attraction was Jack Doyle. He had been matched against Eddie Phillips in a return engagement. What would he do this time?

Most of the contests on that card, as I recall, went their full distance. Knock-outs and similar brief encounters were in short supply that glorious night. Certainly the main event of the evening, Harvey versus McAvoy, travelled its full fifteen rounds.

Now it is a well-known fact that most boxing tournaments commence with the less important bouts, usually termed 'the preliminaries'. These are normally followed by the chief supporting contest, or, as it is known in the States, the semi-final. Then comes the big fight of the evening. When that is over, something of an anti-climax sets in: two unlucky boxers of relative unimportance climb into the ring and wage a bout which is of some consequence to themselves but in which hardly anyone else present is interested. This is the time for post-mortems on the big fight which has just finished, and that period when the hall or stadium slowly begins to empty. If the bout in progress lasts its full six or eight rounds, the unfortunate and unappreciated boxers find that with each succeeding session they are performing before less and less people. It is a traditional occurrence, and one which empties the place gradually. I suppose that its sole virtue is that it prevents too much congestion at the local stations and bus stops.

This time it did not happen. The Doyle versus Phillips contest was nominally the chief supporting bout, and *should* have been staged before Harvey and McAvoy met. Most people were aware of this, and were in their seats and on the terraces in good time. In addition, those monied and upper-crust sportsmen who normally enjoy a good dinner at their leisure before attending these functions and drive in their Rolls-Royces or Bentleys to the scene of events in time to occupy the expensive ringside seats shortly before the principal contest, all

86

seemed to converge upon the White City rather earlier in the evening in order not to miss the antics of Jack Doyle.

The result was that there was a solid traffic-jam half the length of Wood Lane. This caused considerable irritation and apprehension outside the stadium, and quite a bit inside it, too. We, up in the stands, knew nothing of what was going on just at that time, of course, but the promoter did. He was very worried, and for good reason. Jack Doyle, the cause of all the bother, was having difficulty in getting to the White City himself!

As preliminary followed preliminary, and no Doyle was in evidence, it became necessary for those responsible to alter the course of proceedings. By the time Jack Doyle had abandoned his car somewhere near Shepherd's Bush and was dodging through the stationary traffic at a brisk double, Harvey and McAvoy had already been summoned to the ring for their hour-long encounter.

When their contest was over and Harvey had been declared the winner I doubt very much whether more than a dozen people in that vast stadium got up and left. By now I was acutely conscious of the situation, without knowing exactly what had been going on off-stage, so to speak. As the Harvey-McAvoy fight drew to its close it occurred to me that the hour was growing late. I had a long way to go to get home, and I was aware that a large proportion of the some fifty thousand people present would very soon be making a bee-line for the White City station a hundred yards or so up the road.

When the stadium lights went out and the spotlight picked out the tall and resplendent figure of Jack Doyle striding across the turf, accompanied by his new, tiny Mexican film-star wife, Movita, I took a hasty glance at my watch. It said five minutes to eleven. By *eleven o'clock precisely* I was struggling in the vanguard of a good-tempered mob at the gates of White City station, and then easing myself on to the platform! I swear that this is no exaggeration. The fight was that short.

Doyle came out of his corner in his normal style. In a matter of seconds he had shot over a right which sent Phillips to his knees. There was a short count and Phillips was up. Another wild flurry, and down went Phillips again. I don't think he was very badly hurt, but he was certainly shaken. He tottered erect once more, only to face another charge from Doyle. To the shrieks and yells from the fifty thousand onlookers, yet another bludgeoning swipe sent Phillips to the canvas. The whole affair looked to be over, and it nearly was. The rubbery-legged East-ender staggered to his feet, faced his oncoming opponent, and as Jack Doyle rushed in for the *coup de grâce,* Phillips shot out a desperate right to the jaw.

It caught Jack Doyle in full flight. He went down with a bang, flat on his back and with his arms outflung. Not a soul in the arena heard the count, but no count was necessary. After about eight seconds Doyle just raised his head : no more. Then back it fell with a bang, and the fight was over.

I think that only the concerted hilarity of the vast crowd prevented serious damage and injury that night during the general exodus. Jack Doyle had done it again. The long-awaited fight had lasted a matter of seconds rather than minutes, but I doubt if more than a handful of the spectators were disappointed. Doyle had lived up to all expectations.

This occasion marked the end of the Irishman's career as a big time performer in English rings. He did, I believe, fight once or twice in Dublin and district during the war, but the details of these minor contests elude me. He also managed to keep in the news with a little roistering here and there. Inevitably, in the late Forties, he was prevailed upon to turn his talents to the wrestling ring, and for a time he had some success in this endeavour. But Jack Doyle was always a puncher, first and last, and you mustn't – or shouldn't – hit with the closed fist in wrestling.

Today a great many people look back upon Jack Doyle as something of a joke in British boxing. I think of him with fondness. He did his part in keeping alive an interest in domestic pugilism at a time when it was sorely needed. I think he was responsible for selling more tickets at the box office than any fighter of his time. He gave us some disappointing moments, it is true, but he also enlivened many a duff programme by his unpredictability.

From 1932 until the outbreak of war in 1939 he went to the post twenty times. Younger readers may be surprised to learn that he lost on only five of these occasions. Two of these losses were on a disqualification, and he had his man beaten and on the floor the second time when his impetuosity led him to strike the fallen man. Both his fights with Phillips seemed as good as won before the climax. His defeats, of course, netted far more publicity than his victories : he was *not* the perennial loser he is often thought to have been.

The twenty bouts went only a total of forty-six rounds. Apart from the freak twelve-rounder versus King Levinsky, only twice did his engagements go longer than the second round, and no fewer than ten of them ended in the first.

He made quite a fortune in his day. Unlike Billy Walker thirty years later, he spent the lot. It is ironical that had he been wielding his fists at the same time as the aforementioned Walker he could have made yet another fortune in just one fight with that very same gentleman. No stadium in Britain would have been big enough to hold the crowd that wished to see it, and the promoter could have asked his own prices. The outcome of such a meeting we can only guess at, but what an occasion it would have been !

13 Ring Oddities – II

Bob Fitzsimmons was probably the oddest character who ever made a name for himself in boxing. Certainly he was one of the most remarkable. Like many of the other pugs who have not been exactly normal in their appearance, style or accomplishments, his image has had plenty of embellishment. Yet the facts remain, and these are sufficiently unusual to make Fitzsimmons unique.

He was born at Helston, Cornwall, on 4 June, 1862, and for this reason alone he has often been claimed as having been an Englishman. Although there is no gainsaying this fact, his family emigrated to New Zealand with him when he was still a baby. All his boxing and fighting were learned in the Antipodes, and he never put up his fists in Great Britain except in exhibition contests.

He grew to stand just a little under six feet in height. He was lean, knock-kneed, and gangling: the original 'spindle-shanks'. Had he followed a purely sedentary occupation, the chances are that he might never have weighed much more than ten stone in his life. As it happened, he was apprenticed to a blacksmith, and the work he did in his youth helped him to develop enormous and powerful muscles in his arms, back and shoulders. He was *not* built like the proverbial inverted pyramid, as it has so often been claimed, but his upper half was certainly over-developed at the expense of his under-pinnings, and he presented a grotesque figure. At the age of about twenty he weighed a little under eleven stone.

Not only was he top-heavy and awkward-looking, Fitzsimmons was also incredibly ugly. He was a red-head – academically-speaking – but he was a premature baldy. What little hair he retained mostly sprouted in gingerish tufts from his cauli-flower ears. He was also fair-skinned and freckled. The freckles were not confined to his face: they spread across his knotty back and shoulders. Stripped for action, he looked like an elderly red pelican. Small wonder that at first he was a figure of fun.

As an amateur fighter, in New Zealand, he had considerable success. He twice won the championship of his country in competitions organised by the great Jem Mace, and among the men he defeated at this time was the famous Maori heavyweight, Herbert Slade.

Fitzsimmons learned to fight in a hard and rough school. He became a fair enough boxer, but it was the terrific power in his back and shoulders which enabled him to win most of his fights. Between 1880 and 1890 he served a rugged apprentice-ship in New Zealand and Australian rings.

When he sailed for San Francisco in the spring of 1890, he was already twenty-eight years old, which is getting on a bit for a fighter of his weight. He was then a heavy welter, or perhaps a light middleweight. Nobody took him very seriously at first: he was pretty much of an unknown quantity to sporting

California, and besides this he cut such an absurd and strange appearance.

But early in 1891 he won his first world's championship. At New Orleans he faced the original Jack Dempsey, known as 'the Nonpareil', and he knocked out this formidable character in thirteen rounds and took his middleweight title.

At the age of thirty, when most fighters seriously think about retiring, Fitzsimmons was only just getting off the ground in his fantastic flight through pugilistic history. He spent the early eighteen-nineties in knocking over any presumptuous boxer with the temerity to face him. Although he continued to claim the middleweight championship, he put on a little more weight and elected to swap blows with the bigger fellows for more lucrative purses. His sights were now set on Jim Corbett and the heavy-weight championship of the world.

Fitz was a phenomenal puncher. He hit so hard that he, still well under twelve stone, flattened men much heavier than himself. Peter Maher, for example, a knock-out specialist him-self and a hundred-and-ninety-pounder, was never a match for Fitzsimmons.

Late in 1896, Ruby Robert, as the newspapers came to refer to him, completely outclassed Tom Sharkey and then sank a vicious punch into that gentleman's midriff. It literally paralysed Sharkey, and from all accounts it was a perfectly fair blow. But amid scenes approaching a riot, the referee disqualified Fitzsimmons and awarded the fight to Sharkey on a low blow. That the referee happened to be the legendary Wyatt Earp, who was armed at the time, would suggest that the conclusion of this contest might be termed 'unsatisfactory'. Wyatt Earp was a notorious gun-slinger and law-enforcer, but he knew relatively nothing about the finer points of pugilism. He had, in fact, been enlisted to officiate at this contest primarily be-cause of his reputation for intimidation, and because nobody else wanted the job. Most of the betting money was on Sharkey, and when he was sent down grovelling in the eighth round and the crowd yelled loudly that he had been fouled, I believe that Wyatt Earp decided that discretion was the better part of valour. He got the message.

A Burt Lancaster or a Hugh O'Brian, playing this former Dodge City marshal on the screen, would, of course, have yanked out that old equaliser. In the faces of a lynch-crazy mob he would have counted out Tom Sharkey and raised Fitz's arm as the winner. Perhaps someday somebody will make a film showing *this* episode in the career of the famous Wyatt Earp?

In his very next contest, Bob Fitzsimmons, now at the age of thirty-five, and weighing just under twelve stone, won the heavyweight championship of the world by knocking out James J. Corbett in the fourteenth round. It is interesting to note that he accomplished this remarkable feat with a surprise punch identical to the one which had felled Sharkey. This time, however, the referee was not inimidated, and Corbett was counted out. I have dealt with this unique punch, the so-called 'solar plexus blow', in greater detail elsewhere in these pages.

Fitzsimmons now went into semi-retirement, as well he might at that time of life. It was over two years before he boxed seriously again, when he lost his heavyweight title to the mighty Jim Jeffries. He took a pretty bad beating, and it was generally supposed that he would now give up this hazardous occupation altogether. But surprisingly, in the following years he became more active than ever. It was not a case of a veteran pug clinging to the only means of livelihood he knew, long after his best days were over. He really liked a scrap, and he had no pleadings from a fond family for him to give it all up. His wife was almost as pugnacious as himself, and she showed few signs of squeamish feminity at the ringside during his fights. He was also shrewdly managed and advised by his brother-in-law, Martin Julian. It appears to have been an ideal ménage.

The size of his opponents held no terrors for this amazing man. At thirty-eight he could still knock out heavyweights like Ed Dunkhorst, who was known as the Human Freight Car because of his size, and Gus Ruhlin, called the Akron Giant. When he was forty, he even elected to have another shot at Jeffries, in an effort to regain the title. It is said that on this occasion Fitzsimmons put his finger on the scales, so to speak. He reinforced his punching powers by the illegal use of plaster of Paris on his bandages before donning the gloves. He certainly cut Jeffries about quite a bit, but he was facing an almost indestructible champion at the very height of his prowess. Ruby

Robert punched himself to a standstill, and then succumbed to the knock-out in the eighth round.

It was at this period in the history of pugilism that an event occurred which eventually resulted in Bob Fitzsimmons becoming the first man ever to win three world's championships at different weights. While I admit to a tendency to digress at all times, I positively jump at the chance when it is absolutely unavoidable.

For some years the middleweight division had been set at a limit of eleven stone four pounds. Any boxer not able to make this weight on the scales was obliged to try his luck versus heavyweights, and many of these were fourteen or fifteen stone, and sometimes more. Fitzsimmons, of course, had taken this in his stride, but he was unique, because of his freakish build and power. But imagine a man like, let us say, Ray Robinson, having to shape up against a Cassius Clay or a Joe Frazier.

An enterprising boxing promoter and manager named Lou Houseman had the idea that a new division should be established between the middleweights and the big men. He conceived this notion primarily because he guided the fortunes, at that time, of a pretty good boxer named Jack Root, who had outgrown the middleweight poundage. Houseman was wise enough to see that his protégé stood no chance with a man like Jeffries, and he campaigned for the establishment of a new grade, to be called light-heavyweight. In addition to his mangerial jobs, he also happened to be a reporter on a Chicago newspaper, and so had the ideal means of publicising his proposition. Sports editors throughout the country liked the suggestion. The new weight division was established at 175 lb., exactly twelve-and-a-half stone. When it was first adopted in Great Britain we called it cruiserweight – an ideal appellation.

The first light-heavyweight championship match took place at Detroit in April, 1903. The contestants were Kid McCoy and – yes, you've guessed it – Jack Root. Lou Houseman's enterprise paid off : his man won on points.

However, their triumph was short-lived. A few months later, in his first defence of the new title, Root was knocked out by George Gardner. This new champion was no mug within the ropes. He had a good record, but he was ill-advised enough to tackle, in *his* first defence of the championship, old Bob Fitzsimmons, a man with vast experience who had, for years, been gladly giving away weight and more than holding his own with all but the very best.

In November, 1903, now aged forty-one, Fitzsimmons clearly outpointed Gardner to become the first man in the history of boxing to win three world's championships in three separate weight divisions.

Bob Fitzsimmons still had no serious thoughts of retiring permanently from the ring. Exhibitions and work on the stage occupied much of his time, and his physical condition was still better than that of most men half his age. But by now he was almost totally bald. He looked to be in his sixties rather than his forties, and he was more grotesque than ever.

It is true that he fought in earnest very seldom at that time. Despite his general condition, there *was* evidence that he was growing old and rusty, and he knew it. But he could still not give up the more competitive side of his job entirely. He would don his tight, knee-length white shorts, tie his coloured sash about his waist, and climb through the ropes to do battle on the few occasions when the financial inducement seemed to justify it.

In 1905 he was knocked out by Philadelphia Jack O'Brien, and was relieved of his third championship. This was no disgrace : O'Brien was one of the greats of his class and era. But even this reverse could not convince Bob Fitzsimmons that he should now be thinking of the rocking-chair rather than the stool in the corner of a boxing ring. Eighteen months later he took on an up-and-coming young Negro heavyweight, Jack Johnson, who was just beginning to make a name for himself. The owner of that name, hardly ever to be out of the newspapers during the following decade, knocked old Fitz cold in the second round.

1909 found the ever-green pug back in Sydney, New South Wales. Here he fought what was to be the last great battle of his long career. Against the Australian heavyweight, Bill Lang, he put up a magnificent performance before being stretched unconscious in the twelfth round.

And yet *four years later,* in January, 1914, at the age of

fifty-two, the lure of the ring was still there. Bob Fitzsimmons boxed a six rounds 'no decision' fight with one K.O. Sweeney. This engagement brought to an end what must be the most remarkable boxing career of all time, of an odd and unique individual. To paraphrase that immortal ballad, *Eskimo Nell:*

> He performed his trick in a way so slick
> As to set in complete defiance
> The basic cause and the primary laws
> That govern fistic science.

14   Yussel

Joe Jacobs was a shrewd and calculating little boxing manager, a vulpine, cigar-chewing Broadway character who never made a move without first figuring all 'the yangles'. He had no ethics and few loyalties: he would steal another man's fighter for a buck, if he could, and cut his best friend's throat, figuratively, for two. Physically, he was puny and apparently under-nourished, until his last years when he took on a paunch, but mentally he was streets ahead of his fellows all his life. In a dog-eat-dog profession, a grim Disneyland of the big bad wolf and the smiling shark, he was supreme. They called him 'Yussel the Muscle'.

With all his sharpness and acumen, Joe Jacobs had a dis-arming and oddly lovable quality about him. He pulled one or two strokes in his early days that were so outrageous, but with a sheepish grin and a roll of his big cigar, that he became some-thing of a legend in his own life-time. He also coined one or two famous phrases which mistakenly branded him as an illiterate. Sam Goldwyn, a contemporary of his in the equally-competitive film world, made one or two unfortunate *gaffes* and malapropisms in his salad days and thereafter became lum-bered with any *gaucherie* the newspapers cared to hang on to him. 'A verbal contract ain't worth the paper it's written on'

95

was one. Another was : 'I can describe that idea in two words – *Im possible!*' Goldwyn, of course, was responsible for very few of the utterances for which he is attributed. Similarly, little Joe Jacobs never made many of the cracks he is supposed to have made and never perpetrated many of the deals for which he has been blamed.

For all that, he was still the arch-rogue in a profession where roguery abounds, and he was one of the most successful managers of all time. He 'owned' five world champions during his career : an enviable record, and one very, very few pugilistic pilots can match.

The tiniest of his championship charges was Frankie Genaro, an Italian-American flyweight of considerable renown. The National Boxing Association of America recognised his claim to the title, but the New York State Athletic Commission, an influential body, upheld the claim to eminence of Midget Wolgast. When the pair got together to settle the issue they boxed a draw, and settled nothing. Genaro travelled to Europe in 1931, where Jacobs had no influence at the time, and the little champion was unwise enough to tackle a relatively un-known Frenchman named Young Perez, who knocked him out in a couple of rounds.

A little heavier than Genaro was André Routis, a feather-weight from Bordeaux. This young gentleman was a fair enough fighter but a little shy of the first class. He flunked whenever he faced a man in the front rank. When he decided to test his fortunes in the United States, Yussel was on hand to guide his destiny. On achievement, Routis did not merit a chance at the championship when Jacobs induced the mentors of Tony Canzoneri to sign their man for a title fight. Indeed, Canzoneri had already beaten Routis fairly easily over twelve rounds a couple of years earlier, and knew his worth. But Joe Jacobs had 'figgered the yangle' : he had seen that Canzoneri had grown into a lightweight, would have a hard time in reducing to the featherweight poundage of nine stone, and would have great difficulty in boxing fifteen hard rounds against the bustl-ing Routis without tiring. His judgment was right, and his man won. Yussel chortled with glee and rubbed his hands, but his success with the Frenchman was short-lived. Tony Can-zoneri went on to become one of the greatest lightweight cham-

pions of all time; on the other hand, you may be reading of
André Routis here for the first time. He didn't exactly set the
Thames, the Seine, or the Hudson on fire. He lost six of his
subsequent non-title contests, one of which, by the way, was
versus a Tony Canzoneri who didn't have to make nine stone
this time. Routis then lost his championship to Battling Battalino
and passed into limbo. Still, Joe Jacobs had had another 'champion', and had done all right financially.

Yussel also handled the affairs in the United States of two
holders of the light-heavyweight title during the Twenties : Mike
McTigue, an Irishman, and Jack Delaney, a French-Canadian.
He took McTigue down into the deep south of Columbus,
Georgia, in October, 1923, to box a very popular native son
of that state named Young Stribling. On the face of things,
this was a most unwise piece of match-making. The highly-
partisan southern spectators were supporting Stribling to the
last man, and made it perfectly evident that they expected
their darling to receive the verdict. But Jacobs had done a deal
with the referee, whom he had brought along from New York
'to see fair play'. All reports of this contest suggest that Stribling
won it. I have read, variously, that the referee named McTigue
the winner and then hid under the ring until the local police
had managed to clear the stadium, and that he left the scene
of activities hastily without rendering a verdict at all, to prevent
being lynched, and announced McTigue as the victor a couple
of days later when he was out of harm's way. It is difficult to
get to the real truth of the matter. It is certainly a fact that
the record books show this unsavoury affair as a draw, and there
is no doubt at all that both Jacobs and his protégé, McTigue,
were fortunate to leave Columbus without being strung up.
Yussel bluffed his way out, convincing the local authorities that
if anything happened to him his very influential New York
pals would come down and raze Columbus from the map.
The probable truth is that most of his New York acquaintances,
at that time, would have sent a vote of thanks to the state of
Georgia, at least, if Joe Jacobs had been lynched.

The other light-heavyweight champion with whom Jacobs
was, for a time, associated, was the extraordinarily clever Jack
Delaney. Nobody was a true match for him at his weight, and
he was induced to try his luck for the heavyweight honours in

1927. The upshot was disastrous, and he retired the following year after one or two bad beatings.

Joe Jacobs was inordinately partial to the idea of signing up foreign fighters visiting the United States to make their fortunes. He had the contacts to get these men lucrative engagements: fights they could never have obtained without his aid. Further, he knew that the fans were always attracted by a bout with an international flavour to it. That the onlookers were invariably supporting the boxer in the corner opposite to the one in which he was working did not bother him at all. Patriotism, after all, was for suckers. Probably the best day's work he ever did in this facet of his business was his immediate latching-on to a hard-punching but comparatively unknown German heavyweight visitor named Max Schmeling, in 1929.

By judicious matching and skilful publicity he steered his charge through a brief elimination tournament to a fight for the vacant heavyweight championship of the world, which had been left in abeyance when Gene Tunney retired. It was a most hysterical period in professional boxing, and needs some little elucidation. Jack Sharkey, after having shouted 'Foul!' versus Dempsey and then dropping his arms to take a knockout punch to the jaw back in 1927, had fought his way back to prominence by a dubious and unsatisfactory route. He had again claimed foul tactics all through his win over Stribling early in 1929. His just, and perfectly well-deserved defeat of Loughran that same year had been somewhat besmirched by a strange ending. Loughran had taken a blow to the jaw and had immediately turned round and walked to his corner. 'Let me sit down a minute 'til I see where I'm at,' was his remark, which convinced the referee that he was out on his feet: unconscious but still retaining the use of his limbs and tongue. Tommy Loughran was a highly-literate man who would not normally have used such an ungrammatical expression. The referee stopped the fight to save him from possible permanent injury, but such a sudden ending looked all wrong to the crowd. Finally, Sharkey beat Phil Scott, the Englishman, who was the greatest foul-claimer of all time, with a punch which sent Scott writhing to the boards and clutching his groin. Sharkey actually burst into tears when he thought he was going to be disqualified for a low blow. But the referee took the unusual

98

procedure of giving Scott a short respite and then ordered him to continue. But Phil had no further appetite for battle, and heard himself declared the loser amid derisive yells and boos.

Sharkey was not popular, to say the least, but in fairness it must be admitted that he had done more than his share of eliminating. Schmeling, on the other hand, had been matched by Jacobs with only a couple of reputable opponents. These were Johnny Risko and Paolino Uzcudun. He had beaten them both, but the press and public demanded that he should further show his worth. Joe Jacobs squawked loudly that the best interest would be served if the final eliminating bout for the title were an international one, to placate the many thousands of Europeans who believed that America intended to retain the championship at all costs. Yussel's bludgeoning prevailed. Schmeling and Sharkey were matched.

They were pretty evenly-matched, too. We can now see that over fifteen rounds of boxing it would be difficult to say who might have proved the better man. But their fiasco did not extend beyond the fourth. Sharkey whipped in a body punch which was dangerously close to the belt, if not definitely low, and down went Schmeling. Joe Jacobs, with an astuteness he never surpassed, immediately claimed a foul, and did everything but actually climb into the ring. The referee, Jim Crowley, was nonplussed. He had seen no low blow, since Schmeling's back had been towards him. But with the long run of purported fouls and unsatisfactory endings in recent fights, many involving Sharkey, Crowley allowed himself to be bulldozed by Jacobs into disqualifying the American. Max Schmeling became known as the first man to win the heavyweight championship of the world while sitting on the floor. Yussel had chalked up another one.

Max Schmeling redeemed himself the following year by decisively defeating Stribling, who had been expected to win, and in 1932 came the inevitable return fight with Sharkey. It went the full distance, with the consensus of opinion giving Schmeling a very slight edge. However, the officials favoured Sharkey, and it was from their decision that came the two most famous remarks Yussel Jacobs ever uttered.

'We wuz robbed!' snarled the little man when interviewed by the gentlemen of the press. Later, when he had calmed down a little, he remarked ruefully : 'We shoulda stood in bed.'

Jacobs had now lost a champion, but he still had his fighter. The pair of them had an up-and-down time together in the early Thirties. For one thing, Schmeling appeared to have gone over the hill, and to many he looked ready for the scrap-heap. Max Baer, the new young sensation in the heavyweight division, clobbered him into a rubbery-legged puppet before the referee stopped it in the tenth round, and then another big young fellow, an ex-college boy named Steve Hamas, beat him on points and left him a sorry-looking sight. For another thing, Schmeling was now openly hated in the United States. He was a pure-bred German, and Hitler's emerging policies in Europe at that time were not calculated at endearing native sons of the Reich to the large Jewish population of New York City. Many of the boys along Broadway couldn't understand why Joe Jacobs didn't sever relations with this veteran pug who still made his home in Germany and took all of his prize money back with him. For that matter, it seemed strange that a man like Schmeling should still retain the Jewish Yussel as his American manager. Max was an avowed disciple of the Nazi faith – although it would have been sheer suicide had he expressed any other views – and the Hitler Youth Movement looked upon him as a prime example of Aryan manhood.

Nazi Germany, it may be remembered, had the Olympic Games in 1936. They were mounted in Berlin with the express intention of glorifying the Third Reich, and they were a qualified success – but still a success.

Several other big sporting events were put on during the preceding year as a sort of build-up, and one of them came from an invitation to Steve Hamas to travel to Hamburg and box Max Schmeling in a return fight in the German's home town. The financial inducement was too great to ignore, so the international battle was staged.

Hamas didn't stand a chance from the word go. The fight itself was scrupulously fair, but he was beaten psychologically on the day he signed the contract. The vast hall in Hamburg was bedecked from floor to ceiling with Nazi flags, Max Schmeling strode into the ring to a deafening, concerted roar of 'Heils!' from a partisan crowd, and the whole atmosphere was strongly redolent of the swastika and jack-boot. The most fantastic thing about this whole extravaganza was that little Joe Jacobs was there in Max Schmeling's corner!

The reason is ridiculously simple, of course. Joe needed Max, and Max needed Joe. Considerable money was involved on one side, and politics and money were involved on the other. The fact that Jacobs was Jewish was, if not exactly forgotten, certainly ignored on either side.

Before the fight started, there was a grand communal 'Deutschland Uber Alles', with every soul in the stadium shooting his right arm aloft in the fascist salute. Joe Jacobs, a minority of one, did not dissent. After all, discretion is the better part of valour. Quite naturally, he incurred considerable criticism for his action when he returned to the United States. In my opinion, his reported defence is as good as any Goldwynism. 'Ah,' he said, with a sly wink, 'I saluted, but I kept my fingers crossed!'

Schmeling battered Hamas into submission in nine rounds. The loser never fought again. I don't believe that he became particularly disillusioned with fighting as a profession, but he certainly felt that the whole of Nazi Germany had ganged up against him, and it killed his spirit.

The winner, of course, went on to achieve the greatest upset in pugilistic history. Schmeling returned to New York in 1936, with Hitler's blessing, but in America's view as one more sacrificial lamb before the altar of an all-conquering new god. But under the aegis of the non-Aryan Joe Jacobs, he surprisingly and completely routed the hitherto invincible young Joe Louis, another non-Aryan. Neither Jacobs nor Schmeling gained much popularity in the western world for glorifying the Nazi philosophy in the Berlin Olympics year. Still, Yussel managed to justify his activities as 'business', and he struggled through.

James J. Braddock was the heavyweight champion of the world, an ageing pugilist who knew that he had one, or perhaps two, good fights left in him. His main concern was one more lucrative pay-day. He gladly listened to all of Yussel's blandishments and soon signed to fight Schmeling. But it was not long before Joe Louis had battled his way back to prominence, and Braddock was faced with a crucial problem. The odds had it that he would be licked anyway : which challenger, Schmeling or Louis, should he face? Which opponent would net him the most cash? Despite the fact that Madison Square Garden already had his signature to fight Schmeling, as time passed it became increasingly certain that Louis would get the first chance at him. For one thing, the general public were not particularly keen on the idea of Schmeling taking the title back to Nazi Germany; for another, Louis's advisers were only too well aware that if he did, Joe Jacobs and his fighter would never listen to the proposition of a challenge from Louis unless the fight took place in either Hamburg or Berlin and the Negro accepted the very short end of the purse.

Yussel saw which way the wind was blowing and he did his utmost to clinch the chance for his man. But for once in his life he was outfoxed and outgeneralled. Joe Gould, another Jewish manager who was something of a second carbon copy of Jacobs himself, in both appearance and tactics, effected a supreme stroke of business for his veteran champion, Jim Braddock. Baldly and briefly, he consented to disregard the contract he had made with Jacobs for a Schmeling fight, and to give the chance to Louis on the understanding that Braddock would be paid ten per cent of the Negro's earnings for the next ten years !

In due course, Louis knocked out Braddock in Chicago in eight rounds to become the new champion, but not before Joe Jacobs had done everything in his power to stop the fight. When it became obvious to him that this was quite impossible, he still made absolutely certain that his man would fulfil every detail in his part of the bargain.

The papers called it the 'Phantom Fight'. Yussel and Schmeling turned up on time for the scheduled weigh-in, and actually presented themselves at the vast and empty stadium in New York according to the contract, while the opponent, Jim Braddock, was hundreds of miles away training for the Louis fight in Chicago. The courts upheld Joe Jacobs, but his was a hollow victory. Between 1937 and 1947, Joe Louis was the busiest and 'fightingest' champion professional boxing has ever known. His earnings ran into millions, and exactly one tenth of them went to the bank balance of James J. Braddock.

*   *   *

Precisely one year, to the very day, elapsed between Joe Louis's winning of the heavyweight championship and his defence of that title versus the only man who had ever beaten him. Joe Jacobs, this time, didn't do much to make the match. For two years the poker-faced and unloquacious Brown Bomber had been muttering to his mentors : 'Git me S'melin' ,' an utterance which quickly became as famous as Yussel's 'We wuz robbed'.

The fight lasted less than a round, but nobody in the stadium claimed that he hadn't had his money's worth. Louis handed Schmeling the most punishing, decisive and humiliating defeat one first class pugilist ever dealt another. The referee stopped it just after two minutes had elapsed, with the German a battered and almost senseless hospital case.

It was a popular victory everywhere on earth but in Germany. Berlin radio went off the air seconds after the fight was over, while their newspapers claimed that Schmeling had been deliberately fouled. I have seen the film of this brief bout in slow motion many times, and the truth is as follows : Max had his back to the ropes and was taking a vicious and sustained beating about both the head and body. The punches which Louis whipped in were so powerful that Schmeling, who was unable to retreat, actually turned his back upon his opponent at the very moment the champion sent in a vicious right to the body. It caught Schmeling in the spine and he drooped over the ropes. It was *not* a deliberate kidney blow, although it is not surprising that Joe Jacobs and others made such a claim. In fact, an X-ray photograph revealed that the punch had actually chipped one of Schmeling's vertebrae.

There is a Yussel story to this fight, like many others in which he had a hand, which I have always thought too good to be true. It concerns one Arno Hellmiss, an unpleasant and arrogant Nazi sports commentator, who had travelled to New York to cover the whole affair for German radio. The story goes to the effect that for weeks he made himself disliked by his perpetual glorification of Germany and his persistent needling of the Jewish Joe Jacobs. After Schmeling's humiliation, he is said to have fled from the scene of combat to seek solace in a bar near the docks, waiting for the first boat to take him back home. Here Joe Jacobs found him, although we are not told how or why. At all events, the story continues that Jacobs, who had been belittled and insulted by Hellmiss for weeks, was the only man who would drink and sympathise with the German. Further, when Hellmiss became violently ill, and was escorted on to a ship bound for Germany, only Yussel was there to tend the stricken man. Eventual medical diagnosis proved that Helmiss had been slipped a Mickey Finn, which is a purgative about as strong as a horse pill.

After the news got around and about, Jacobs was quite naturally accused by certain characters as being the one responsible for the administering of the pill. 'What, me?' said Yussel. '*Me* give that guy a Mickey Finn? Why, I liked him. I slipped him *three!*'

Having lost his main meal-ticket, Jacobs did not exactly starve. He turned his attentions elsewhere among his protégés, and now began the build-up of a rough-house bruiser in his second string who had already been battling with indifferent success for a good ten years. Tony Galento was a short and rotund Italian-American from New Jersey who loved to fight but who hated to train. He weighed as much, or more, than most heavyweights, but a lot of his poundage was concentrated in his prodigious midriff. It was said that his favourite diet was hot dogs and beer, and Jacobs did nothing to deny this belief. He encouraged it.

Galento won very few of his contests on points: he either knocked his man kicking in a few rounds or took a licking himself. He was far from invincible, but nobody liked fighting him. He used his head, thumbs, elbows and – occasionally – his knees. In a bar-room brawl where anything goes he was a world champion, but in a boxing ring, hampered by padded gloves and niceties like three-minute rounds, rules and a referee, his style was cramped. Galento was a million miles from a chance at Joe Louis and the supreme honours until Joe Jacobs turned his full attention to the fortunes of the cart-horse in his stable.

Within a year, by the use of the most outrageous ballyhoo, Yussel bulldozed the public into actually believing that his walking beer barrel stood an even chance with Louis. Galento himself, in spite of his record, had never doubted it. True, Tony did his part in the campaign by knocking over several well-known heavyweights, but they were hardly ranking contenders. Joe Louis had, in fact, already softened up four of them well before Jacobs matched his man against them. Yussel steered well clear of any challenger who might have upset his well-laid plans.

By this time, Galento had been dubbed Two-Ton Tony, and was taken to the hearts of the general public. Like any fighter worth his salt, he had unlimited confidence in himself, but he expressed nothing but contempt for the prowess of his prospective opponent. Punching was his trade, and he had left-hooked so many lesser men into oblivion that he really believed that he could serve the great Brown Bomber likewise. 'I'll moider da bum,' became the popular catch-phrase of 1939.

Jacobs fanned the flames of publicity. His efforts succeeded in attracting an enormous crowd of fans who bought tickets with the confident expectation that Louis would rout his presumptuous challenger, but also with the hope that the fat little man would somehow make good his boasts. Galento's logic was simple and unreasonable, but quite unarguable and therefore irrefutable.

'Louis is a bum,' I recall his informing a reporter who interviewed him.

'But how can he be?' asked the journalist. 'He's the greatest fighter of modern times. He's knocked out five former world champions and beaten every man who took a chance with him. What have you got to say to that?'

Galento thought for a moment. 'Louis is a bum,' he said.

The great Brown Bomber, of course, punched Two-Ton Tony to a wobbling hulk in four rounds, but not before Galento had proved that he and his manager were not all talk and nothing else. In the second round the paunchy challenger let fly with a left-hook at the same moment that Louis attempted an identical blow. Galento beat the champion to the punch and dumped him on to his buttocks. The Negro then proved his true greatness by getting up and not only staving off the finisher but by ending the round in the better condition of the two.

Galento was a little ungracious after the fight, in my opinion, throwing the blame for his defeat on Joe Jacobs. 'That's the last time I fight the way my manager tells me,' he informed the movie cameramen in his dressing-room. 'From now on I fight my own fight. I like to give one, take one, then sling one over an' knock 'im dead.' He wiped his battered face with a towel. 'I had him down twice,' he added as an afterthought.

He was wrong there, just as he was wrong in his previous explanation for his defeat. There was no evidence that he fought in any way other than that in which he always waged battle: to go in and slug it out until he or the other man was beaten.

Not so very long afterwards, when Joe Jacobs died, the story that circulated had a very different ring. Trilby-Tony had lost his Svengali. 'Joe, Joe,' Galento is purported to have wailed at his manager's graveside, 'whattam I gonna do with these two fists now?' Two-Ton Tony need not have worried: he was finished as a front-rank performer well before that.

When Yussel shuffled off this mortal coil there were more than a few sighs of relief, but one or two sentimental tears were also shed along that strip of New York City known as Jacobs's beach. With all his faults he had a spark of genius with his cunning moves and opportunism. More than a little of the colour and glamour went out of boxing when Joe Jacobs died.

15   Computerised Fights

Many years ago, when I first started buying boxing magazines, the contributors always seemed to be naming their 'Best of All Time'. Their choices differed, of course, but you could always bet that Johnson, Jeffries or Dempsey would be one of those nominated. Later on, when Joe Louis appeared, he, too, was included in the act. A few years afterwards, Rocky Marciano was often awarded the accolade. In more recent times, Cassius Clay appeared to be a frequent favourite.

This game is a popular one among boxing writers. When

they grow tired of it, or when there is nothing else they can think of to write about, they concoct their 'Dream Contest'. This is accomplished by taking two great champions of different eras – men who never met in the ring – and by writing a wholly fictitious account of what would have happened had they met each other.

Naturally, the fight is always a classic. It is never over and done with in a round or two, and it never goes the full distance to be decided on points. It is never dull or disappointing, and it is always a magnificent and courageous struggle. It always has plenty of thrills and knock-downs, with the issue ever in doubt. Eventually, after about ten or a dozen rounds, it culminates in a thrilling knock-out. The winner, of course, is the fighter the particular writer happens to favour as the 'Greatest of All Time' at the particular moment.

Whenever two very highly-rated boxers do happen to meet somewhere near the peak of their careers, the outcome is often well below expectations. Liston and Clay are two prime examples. And occasionally one of the select nominees, at a moment when he is coming, faces another of the old favourites, when *he* is going. You get a result, of course, but more often than not the fight is a travesty. Jeffries, after six years in retirement, should never have been allowed in the same ring with Johnson. Similarly, when Marciano knocked out Louis, he was beating the equivalent of a fifth carbon copy of the Brown Bomber of ten years previously.

Still, the game goes on. Particularly when real life 'Battles of the Century' are in short supply, 'Dream Contests' continue to be reported, and they do little harm. They help to sell a few copies of the periodicals in which they appear and they make interesting reading, even if they make little money.

Then came the idea for putting this business on a financial basis in today's age of technology. According to accounts, the first idea involved feeding data into computers to produce the 'All-Time Heavyweight Champion', with nation-wide broadcasts over sound radio in the United States. Rocky Marciano came out on top, but the effusive and touchy Cassius Clay took exception to this result. He claimed that he and Marciano, both undefeated champions, had not met in the fictional computer tournament. He even sued for a million dollars damages!

(Can you imagine anything like this happening elsewhere than in the United States? Further, can you imagine anyone other than Cassius Clay attempting it?) Clay won his case, but was awarded one dollar damages!

A hollow victory? Not by any means. The story goes that Clay wanted a computerised fight versus Marciano as well, to settle the issue. The probable facts are that by this time, with all the publicity that had accrued, it was decided that since both Clay and Marciano were still young enough to pass, a filmed battle between the pair could make a fortune for all concerned. Both were in retirement, and Marciano had not fought seriously for thirteen years, but that was no obstacle. The financial inducement was sufficient to send him into intensive training in order to reduce his bulk to something like the poundage at which he had once fought.

Over an extended period, behind locked doors, and under conditions of highly-publicised secrecy, Clay and Marciano boxed an amazing number of abbreviated rounds according to the dictates of the computer. Plenty of phoney blood was in evidence, mostly supposed to be coming from Marciano, canned audience reaction was turned up or down as occasion demanded, and each punch was clearly heard as it landed, or appeared to land, with that dubious monotony of glove into punching-bag that one always gets in dramatised fight films but which never sounds quite the same in genuine scraps. For all that, the two of them really appeared to be having a go, and I have not the slightest doubt that more than a few honest-to-goodness digs were actually exchanged. The whole thing was quite entertaining so long as you did not take it too seriously.

I have read that they boxed no fewer than seven alternative endings. It seems that only the director, the producer and a few technicians were aware of the actual outcome before this contest was seen by the public. Even the contestants did not know who was supposed to have won the fight. As a point of interest, Rocky Marciano was killed in a plane crash after the filming but before the editing and public screening, and he died not knowing who was the current 'greatest'.

Copies of the film were shown simultaneously throughout the United States. A further copy was flown to London and was exhibited on television some twenty-four hours later in

Britain. Of course, the press had a wonderful field-day, beautifully ruining the whole thing for British viewers by reporting the result of the fight in the evening editions of the newspapers some hours before it was shown on the domestic screen.

Rocky Marciano knocked out Cassius Clay in the thirteenth round. We are invited to believe that this is what would have happened had these two admittedly great pugilists met at the height of their abilities, because this is, we were told, what the computer said would have happened.

I have nothing against computers, as such. But I have a considerable bias against the human element involved – operators are human, and fallible, as I know to my cost. I concede that there is a strong possibility that a Rocky Marciano of, say, 1950, would have knocked out a Cassius Clay of, perhaps, 1966. And yet the very reverse might have been true. And remember, Clay was a coloured man, and not precisely popular in his own country at the time, while Marciano was white, and had never been anything else than popular anywhere. Also remember, they boxed seven alternative endings. I confess to being more than a trifle cynical about this whole business. We have been so brain-washed by the magic word 'computer' that the general tendency is to accept it as synonymous with the word 'infallible'. In my youth I first heard that overworked expression: 'The camera cannot lie'. It had a certain ring and irrefutable logic about it: I then accepted the phrase as gospel. But nobody said that the camera was not itself limited in what it depicted by the skill or otherwise of the operator.

16 The Greatest Fight I Ever Saw

Once or twice in every few years two boxers of approximately equal weight rise from the ranks to championship class or status and so capture the imagination of all lovers of sport that a meeting between the pair becomes known as a 'natural'. It is essential on such occasions that the participants should be pretty near the peak of their prowess. Preferably, each should boast a string of impressive successes in his immediately previous record. The impending battle then takes on the colour of a Napoleon versus Wellington clash. Sometimes it's the case of the irresistible force meeting the immovable object, when, in the words of the song, 'something's gotta give'. On other occasions, the height and weight of the protagonists are not as even as they should be, ideally, as in the case of Tom Sayers versus John C. Heenan, the last great international bare-knuckle fight, in 1860, and in that of Georges Carpentier versus Jack Dempsey, the so-called 'Battle of the Century', in 1921. Then, of course, you get the flavour of David and Goliath, with all of the public's sympathies with the smaller man and most of its money on the big 'un.

Among well-remembered contests between evenly-matched big fellows, there is the famous Peter Jackson-James J. Corbett bout, which was *so* close and even that each nullified the other's efforts, so that it came to no satisfactory conclusion at all. Many years later we had Cassius Clay versus Sonny Liston. Their two meetings promised much but produced little. The lighter divisions have tended to produce naturals which came up to their expectations. Among these smaller men I can think of contests whose box-office appeal sent crowds rushing to buy tickets: the Benny Lynch-Peter Kane bout at Glasgow, Stanley Ketchel versus Billy Papke, Ad Wolgast and Battling Nelson, that marathon series of fights between Jack Britton and Ted 'Kid' Lewis, and the Barney Ross-Tony Canzoneri fights. Yet that inevitable clash in 1939 between Eric Boon and Arthur Danahar led sports writers to run out of adjectives and superlatives.

This contest meant little or nothing outside Great Britain at the time, and today it appears to be all but forgotten everywhere. Yet although it did not draw the receipts that some of the other above-mentioned fights made, I venture to suggest that it passed them all in quality. As far as I am concerned, no other lightweight battle of the twentieth century displayed so much scientific boxing, dogged courage, hard punching and thrills as did that great championship bout on 3 February, 1939. It had everything.

For many months before, its possibility had been discussed in the newspapers and sporting periodicals, and as each man continued to win his fights impressively we knew that Boon and Danahar *must* meet between the ropes before very long. As much as anything else, its attractiveness lay in the extreme dissimilarity, in almost every way, of the two lads concerned.

Eric Boon was short, muscular and chunky, a counter-puncher with enormous strength and devastating power in his fists; Arthur Danahar was tall and slim, a superlative text-book boxer. Boon was a country boy from Chatteris; Danahar was a cockney from Bethnal Green. The one had been a rugged professional from the age of sixteen, learning his trade with wins, losses and draws in small halls; the other had been a brilliant amateur, attracting much attention when he won the A.B.A. lightweight title in 1937, and had boxed only fourteen times as a professional. Boon was managed by the shrewd East-ender, Jack Solomons, who had built his protégé to championship status at the Devonshire Club, in Hackney, and then in association with Sydney Hulls, at Harringay Arena; Danahar had early been taken under the wing of the gentlemanly Jack Harding and the National Sporting Club, and had boxed almost exclusively at their headquarters in the Empress Hall, Earl's Court.

Of the two, Boon was by far the more experienced man, but Danahar was a wizard with the gloves and had boxed his fourteen contests in 1938 without a defeat.

In December of that year, Eric Boon had knocked out Dave Crowley for the British lightweight title, after having been on the receiving end of the exchanges for most of the bout. It was his enormous stamina and dogged courage in the face of adversity, his stubborn never-say-die attitude culminating in the pay-off knock-out punch, which led him to become the most popular box-office attraction among little men in this country for many years. It was after he had deposed the experienced Crowley in thirteen rounds, with his manager now in a position to command the larger end of any prospective purse that we knew that his long-awaited fight versus Arthur Danahar must surely come about within a month or two.

Strictly speaking, Danahar had not boxed or beaten enough really first-class men to warrant his meeting Boon for the championship, and I should say that Ronnie James, Jimmy Vaughan and Johnny McGrory were three contemporary lightweights who deserved a title fight before the Bethnal Green boxer. Danahar had never boxed more than eight rounds at a time during the whole of his professional career, and there was considerable doubt whether he had the staying power to last a gruelling championship fight of fifteen rounds with a man like Boon.

But the public wanted to see the super-stylist Danahar against the hard-punching and all-action Boon. This fight was a natural, if ever there was one; besides, Danahar was still growing, and he gave evidence that he would not be staying in the lightweight ranks for very much longer. If he was ever to take that title, it was now or never.

Since the Board of Control gave its blessing, Syd Hulls lost no time in matching the pair for Harringay Arena. Now John Harding, of Earl's Court and the National Sporting Club, would have loved to have staged this fight at the West London hall, since he had been directly responsible for the developing of Arthur Danahar into a title contender. But neither he nor the N.S.C. were prepared to stand in the boy's way, and they saw their darling bravely enter the enemy's camp, so to speak. This would be the first time Danahar had boxed at Harringay, his opponent's home ground, and apart from one or two of his earlier contests, almost the first time he had appeared professionally before any other than the Earl's Court crowd.

It was rumoured that tickets to this fight of fights would be split up between Earl's Court regulars and those who had consistently followed Boon at the Devonshire Club and Harringay. Although I was a fairly regular attender at Syd Hulls's promotions at the North London arena and had visited the N.S.C.'s Empress Hall weekly soirées on several occasions I was more than a little cynical about this announcement. Besides, I realised that such a crowd of fight fans would rush for the cheaper seats that I made no attempt to apply when the match was made. In my impecunious youth, as an apprentice commercial artist, even a six-shilling ticket took a substantial amount from my weekly wage packet: the contemplation of a more expensive one was quite out of the question. I told myself that I stood no chance at all. It would be like trying to get hold of a Cup Final ticket.

I resigned myself to hearing the contest described over the radio. Television was at that time in its infancy, although, as a point of interest, the bout's appeal led to the very first pioneer effort in this country of beaming a televised fight to West End cinemas and theatres – and at exorbitant prices.

One Saturday morning, about a fortnight before the event was due to take place, my old man – the greatest procrastinator of all time – casually asked me if I intended to witness it, and hinted that he was ready to supply the money if I could get him a seat as well. I replied that I doubted very much if, at this late stage, we could possibly get in, but his own interest imbued me with a sudden new enthusiasm for this forthcoming contest, and I said that I would try to get a couple of tickets in the West End. At noon that day I went to Syd Hulls's headquarters and asked if there were any tickets available.

'All gone,' I was told. Although I had felt that this was inevitable, my heart sank, and I cursed. But then came a ray of hope.

'The only chance you've got,' the clerk said, 'is to apply by post immediately, and take your chance with everybody else.' This was a different answer entirely. 'The tickets haven't been issued yet . . .'

It seemed a slim chance at such a date, I knew, but I wrote off that afternoon, determined now to try anything. I was more than surprised, about a week later, to receive a registered envelope containing two of those precious pink tickets, and never have I been so pleased to receive an envelope as I was that one. I may appear extraordinarily naïve, I know, but it still seems to me that Syd Hulls, with a strict fairness for which I shall ever respect him, had waited until all applications for entrance had arrived, and had then painstakingly chosen from among the thousands of applicants those fans who had regularly written to him for tickets to his earlier promotions. I can think of no other explanation for my good luck.

Good luck it was. People I knew who had never been to Harringay, Earl's Court or the Devonshire Club were offering what seemed fantastic sums for tickets to this fight. I was looked upon as something of a wonder-man for not only having in my possession two of those valuable slips, but for having obtained them at their right price. The speculators had a wonderful evening in Green Lanes and vicinity on the night the contest was held. For long after the fight took place my acquaintances were amazed to hear that I had actually witnessed the Boon-Danahar classic, and I used to think that had the promoter waited until summer and staged the fight at the White City or at another big open-air stadium he could have more than doubled his receipts and set up a new record in this country for boxing crowds. Now I am not so sure : as I say, Danahar wasn't going to stay a lightweight for very much longer. By delaying for a few months, this natural would have been lost.

All this excitement, remember, was brought about not by two big men in the heavyweight division, but by a couple of lads weighing less than ten stone apiece, one of whom was nineteen and the other in his twentieth year!

Blasé sports writers almost went hysterical over this unique pair, and some of the things they wrote will remain great tributes to the two boys who fought it out at Harringay. The *Evening Standard* expert, old Ben Bennison, penned one of his flowery articles in the souvenir programme, and finished :

> ... tonight Hulls will put the coping stone on his activities at Harringay with the most arresting lightweight fight staged in this country for years. In the mightiness of its appeal there has been nothing like it.

Bennison was a great admirer of Arthur Danahar's skill, and he predicted a world's championship for the young cockney almost before he had turned professional.

Trevor Wignall, the *Daily Express* columnist, and the most widely-read of all British sports reporters, contributed a grand article revolving about the father of Syd Hulls and one or two great lightweight fights of the past, and wrote the following paragraph, which sticks in my mind :

> It is more than forty years since I first walked into a booth to watch men swing their gloved fists. I have travelled far, and seen much since then. I have looked on champions as they rose to the heights, and as they fell. Isn't it odd that I think of tonight's contest between Eric Boon and Arthur Danahar as one of the most remarkable in my

experience? It is remarkable because the couple who figure in it are still almost of schoolboy age. They are not yet fully celebrated outside this country, yet they have caused more talk, created more discussion, and been the means of selling more tickets than any other lads of their poundage in the whole history of British boxing.

With so much enthusiasm occurring before the fight took place, one might almost have expected another complete flop. Much-publicised matches have a knack of ending disappointingly, but that battle of Boon and Danahar surpassed the expectations of everybody.

When the pair entered the ring on the evening of Thursday, 3 February, 1939, I would not have bet a penny either way on the result of the match. I knew Boon's capabilities, up to a point, since I had seen him often, but Danahar, apart from his reputation, was something of an unknown quantity. For this reason alone I rather expected the young champion to win, but I do not say that I was supporting him in favour of the challenger. My father, however, was rooting for Danahar from start to finish. Apart from a natural tendency to support the underdog, he appreciated science and cleverness more than strength and force. I always suspected that this dated back twenty years previously, when his national pride had been severely hurt by the rugged Joe Beckett's inglorious display against the Frenchman, Carpentier. In addition, his one glimpse of Eric Boon in action had not been impressive. That had been a few months earlier, when one Mitso Grispos, a relatively unknown Greek, had taken Boon the full distance and besmirched a long run of sensational wins.

Eric Boon looked wonderfully fit when he entered the ring. I think he must have been one of the best-muscled lightweights who ever fought, and his nine stone nine pounds were well distributed over his five feet four inches of height. Arthur Danahar, standing five feet eight, looked an undeveloped stripling by comparison, but he weighed approximately the same as the champion. With arms outstretched to left and right from his body, his reach from finger-tip to finger-tip was seventy-one inches, five more than that of the stocky Boon. It was this advantage that the Londoner meant to use to the full. He was reputed to have the finest straight-left in the business, and it was obvious that this fight would be a match between that long, snaky arm which whipped out with such amazing speed, and the powerful, soporific hooks of Boon.

Danahar looked too frail for a hard tussle when he removed his gown, but he soon dispelled any illusions as to his robustness once the fight was under way. He took some good blows from the champion early on, but he never faltered once. Boon crouched in an attitude which kept him ever ready to deliver a knock-out blow with either fist. Sometimes he stood with his right shoulder foremost, preparing to hook his left in an arc, and sometimes he presented his left shoulder to Danahar, with his right glove hovering ready for a devastating swing to the jaw.

The East-ender never varied in his style. Standing upright, his weight evenly distributed upon the balls of both feet, he held both gloves together at his chest. Many times his left fist streaked out unerringly to Boon's face, and the champion's defence was seldom good enough to deflect it. And now and again Danahar would follow up his lightning leads with a hard right to the body. He came in with those rib-benders with such power and speed that it soon became obvious that all the hard punching did not come from one direction. Then Boon would hook with either fist in an attempted counter-punch, and although he landed several times he failed to catch Danahar on a vital spot. The rounds passed according to the same pattern, with the Bethnal Green boy compiling a generous lead of points.

Up to the seventh round Eric Boon did not once gain the upper hand, and it looked as though his crown was slipping. His eye swelled and closed with the perpetual battering from Danahar's accurate left, and yet he was still as strong as ever. He knew that his opponent had never boxed seriously for longer than eight rounds, and he waited patiently for a sign of weakness.

Danahar began to tire in the eighth. To the onlooker he presented little difference, but Boon recognised the signs and symptoms, and he suddenly and unexpectedly shot across a hook

116

to the jaw which surprised the challenger. It sent him to his haunches as a great shout arose. I studied Danahar closely at this point. He looked more shaken than hurt, and it was apparent that his mind was quite clear. He had been told to take full advantage of the count in the event of such an occurrence, and he looked towards his corner to show that he knew what was going on. He arose before the final drop of the referee's arm and backed away from Boon, but the little champion saw victory in sight and tore into Danahar with both fists flying. The Londoner backed away rapidly, jabbing out that left with amazing accuracy, but before the end of the round Boon connected again, and down went Danahar once more.

But the challenger could take it, and again he arose little the worse. He shot out that piston-like left arm again and again, and seldom did he fail to connect. He held the charging champion well away until the end of the round. Boon hooked and swung desperately, but he could not land with a big one again. But the tables had now turned with a vengeance, and bets were being made on Boon to score a knock-out. This was the first round he had taken, so far, and he was still strong and full of fight, whereas Danahar now began to show definite signs of weariness.

Both men went hard at it in the ninth and tenth rounds. Boon forced the pace with spirited charges which sent Danahar on the defensive and had the crowd on its feet with excitement, but the challenger skilfully avoided those punishing fists and sent across some useful blows to the head which had his man stumbling. Once in each round he surprised everyone by sending Boon to the canvas for short counts, but the champion was unhurt, and the second knock-down came mainly from the ropes catching him behind the legs and unbalancing him. He half fell out of the ring, but pulled himself back almost immediately and renewed his ferocious attack. His blood was up and he was fighting better than ever.

In the eleventh round he seemed to grow even stronger. Although those lefts still streaked out and caught him regularly, they now appeared to be having little effect on him. He shook them off and pounded Danahar around the ring for most of that hectic round and finally sent him to the boards with a terrific clout full on the jaw. This time Danahar was really hurt : you could see it from the glazed look in his eyes. I doubt very much whether he could have arisen in time to continue, but the bell came to his rescue. It cut through the referee's count and the deafening yells which now filled the arena, but only those closest to the ring heard it. Danahar's seconds dragged him to his corner and worked frantically to prepare him for another round.

The excitement throughout that hall now was something I have never witnessed before or since. The pendulum was definitely swinging in favour of Boon, yes, and that early lead of Danahar's had been wiped out, but time was running short. The champion's face was in a pretty bad state, and he could see from only one eye. *He* was tiring too, now, but he could not afford to coast along. Only four rounds remained. He *had* to score a knock-out.

The Bethnal Green boxer came out for the twelfth very slowly. He could hardly summon the strength to put his fists up, and the muscles of his legs were fluttering, but he was still determined to do his best. He was banking on a close points victory if he could last the battle through. Moving round and round the ring, he still had little difficulty in landing on Boon's face with that left glove, and those blows scored points, but there was little power behind the punches. As the round progressed, and the wary Boon stalked him, he grew slower and slower. It became apparent that it was now just a case of how long he could last. Twice more he fell during this session, and each time he had difficulty in arising.

Everyone was amazed at the challenger's wonderful display of courage. Tottering around the ring, his strength drained from him and his legs wobbling, he still pathetically pushed out his now ineffective left fist. Only Danahar's own unsteadiness prevented the half-blind Boon from landing the accurate finisher he was trying so hard to send across.

Danahar went to the boards three times in round thirteen, and each time his spirit alone dragged him erect. He knew little of what was going on, I am sure, and was now boxing purely from instinct. As the almost-exhausted Boon still came in with his ceaseless attacks, the losing man's fist moved out automatically. It was pitiful to watch that famous straight-left go out from his shoulder slowly and without the strength behind it to hold away a child. It barely reached Boon's head, who had no difficulty in brushing it aside and smashing wild and erratic counter blows in the direction of Danahar's jaw. Some of them landed, but still the challenger would not stay down!

In the interval some of the spectators called loudly to the referee to stop the fight, but no move was made in this direction, and at the bell others roared for the courageous Londoner to stick it out to the end. But this fourteenth round was the last. Although Danahar had recovered somewhat during the minute's respite, he had neither the power nor the necessary clarity of mind to ward off Eric Boon's final desperate onslaught. Danahar took a punch on the chin which sent him flat on to his back with a bang. The referee stepped in and stopped the contest, waving Boon to his corner. But even in this moment of defeat, Arthur Danahar still made an effort to get up and continue. His seconds were inside the ring in a moment, and he was aided to his corner, and Boon was declared the winner on a technical knock-out in the fourteenth round. The most exciting bout I have ever seen was over.

17   A Sequel

It is ironical that although that Boon-Danahar classic of 1939 was the most inspiring battle between two boxers that I ever witnessed, perhaps the most pathetic stinker I had the misfortune to see was between the same two men.

After that rip-roaring contest in those far off, worrying days just preceding the war, it was inevitable that everyone should look forward to a return bout between these two youngsters. As it happened, we had to wait some six years.

For one thing, although both of these lads were still growing, Danahar had had quite a little trouble in keeping down to the lightweight limit in February, 1939, and a couple of months later, when he was again seen in a ring, he appeared a different person entirely. Whereas he had looked a slim, under-nourished boy when opposing Boon, now he was a man, well-covered and mature, a natural welterweight. When I watched him out-point Harry Craster I did not think I was looking at the same boxer. He now had his sights on Ernie Roderick and the heavier championship. In fact, later that same year, he outpointed Roderick over ten rounds in a non-title bout before his favourite Earl's Court crowd.

For another thing, the war intervened to upset a great many careers, both athletic and otherwise. Professional boxers continued to perform, of course, as did footballers, cricketers and runners. Sport was a great morale-booster during the war, and every effort was made by those in authority to enable top-line entertainers to continue their peace-time occupations. Most of them were in the forces, of course, many of them retaining peak fitness as physical training instructors, and they were granted generous leave from their units to fulfil an engagement. Yet there was never any absolute certainty that the men billed would actually appear. I can recall many occasions, for instance, when I would travel considerable distances to see particular fights in various parts of the country, only to find that one of the advertised principals was being replaced by a last-minute substitute.

During hostilities between 1939 and 1945 the paths of Boon and Danahar did not cross, although each remained active. Boon continued as a lightweight right up to 1944, when he lost his title to Ronnie James. Weakness in reducing to nine stone nine pounds was responsible, as much as anything else, for his defeat. He then entered the welterweight ranks, and took out a new lease on his fighting life. Danahar, meanwhile, boxed his way to a bout for the welterweight championship, but was unfortunate in that the reigning holder was one of the finest combination boxer-fighters of the century when his title was at stake. Although Danahar had previously outpointed Ernie Roderick over ten rounds, things proved very different in a championship contest over the full fifteen rounds.

In 1946, on the first important peace-time promotion bill, Boon was immediately paired with Danahar in the chief supporting contest to the famous Mills-Lesnevich meeting. By this time Jack Solomons had forsaken managing fighters and was well on his way to becoming Europe's biggest boxing promoter. Eric Boon, his former protégé, was now under the wing of Benny Huntman.

After their magnificent contest of 1939, quite naturally the whole country expected something really unusual from this pair in their second engagement. But the upshot was that practically nothing was seen at all. Each had a healthy respect for the other: Boon had no intention of walking continually into that ramrod straight-left, and Danahar was reluctant to lead for fear of those murderous retaliatory counters.

For three-and-a-half rounds they fiddled at arm's length, each waiting for the other to make a decisive move, and they did hardly anything. The spectators were just beginning to settle back and start discussing with one another what a wonderful fight the first one had been by comparison, when the climax came with startling suddeness. I am quite sure that half of those present missed the first solid punch of the bout completely. I know the movie cameraman did. Maybe he had been told to save his film stock for the big fight later on; maybe he took his thumb off the cable release to have a chat with a colleague. Whatever the answer, the film exhibited in the cinemas a day or two later abruptly showed Danahar sitting bewilderedly on the floor of the ring, wondering what had hit him.

He got up after a long count, and the most charitable thing I can say is that he just didn't know what was going on. Boon came in, there was a flurry of arms, and then *down went Boon,* squirming and grimacing, with both hands clutched to his groins! At the ringside: pandemonium. From everywhere else in the arena came cat-calls, whistles and boos. The referee, after some considerable hesitation, announced Danahar as the victor, and this long-awaited return fight was over.

Eric Boon did not leave the ring under his own power. His manager took him on to his shoulders and rode him back to his dressing-room 'piggy back'. Boon really looked as if he wouldn't walk again for a week, at least. Fortunately, the effects of that punch below the belt had no lengthy effects. Shortly afterwards, he took his place in a seat a couple of rows behind me, fully-dressed and apparently in no way inconvenienced, to watch that great battle between Freddie Mills and

Gus Lesnevich. This particular fight, by the way, turned out to be the most exciting scrap I had watched since the original Boon-Danahar classic.

Eric Boon and Arthur Danahar were both great pugilists in 1939. What each might have accomplished had not the war intervened none of us will ever know. In my opinion, Boon was never the same man after he went over the top of a motor-cycle in a country lane, when he was a member of the forces in the early Forties. Danahar, when he faced his old rival the second time, was already suffering from the chest complaint which was to cut his career short within a matter of several months.

I would like to excuse that second meeting. I place it here only as a matter of comparison to their great fight in 1939: the finest contest between two great pugilists I have ever had the privilege to witness.

18   Fight Films

The development of the motion picture camera and the popularisation of glove-fighting occurred at around about the same time – during the last decade of the nineteenth century. Although one or two of the earliest great Queensberry contests were never recorded on celluloid, we are fortunate in that almost every really important contest waged under modern rules and conditions has been filmed.

It was on 7 September, 1894, two years to the day after James J. Corbett had beaten John L. Sullivan to become the first heavyweight champion with the gloves, that the earliest successful motion pictures of a boxing match were shot. An attempt had been made, some time before, to film an actual ring combat, but the conditions had been unfavourable. Corbett was then approached to box a special six-round contest with one Peter Courtney, and he readily agreed. But the stipulation was made that the fight must take place in the studios of the Kinetoscope Company, which were at the Edison Works in Orange, New Jersey. Corbett was also asked to 'carry' Courtney for the six rounds and then to knock him out in the last. This was an arrangement to which he also agreed, since Corbett was far in advance of Courtney in every respect within the ropes.

Later on, when newsreel films of big fights were a regular feature, and the boxers' percentages of the profits from the public showings surpassed the size of the purses in some cases, it often became the thing for a champion to let a fight last a few rounds in order to heighten the value of the movies. This sort of understanding was particularly prevalent when it was obvious to those most intimately concerned that a champion could knock his opponent out with little more than one punch. It is interesting to note that here, in the very first moving pictures of a boxing match, that which was to become a quite frequent happening was put into practice immediately.

The only actual eye-witnesses to the Corbett-Courtney farce were the technicians and one or two favoured guests. The affair went according to plan. I have been fortunate enough to see this pioneer effort, and the champion gave a masterly, if light-hearted, exhibition of scientific boxing, with a smile on his face for most of the time, and then brought over his right to put Courtney down and out almost as the last few feet of film ran through the gate of the camera.

These early fight pictures were a great success, and a naïve public flocked to see them. This 'contest' is actually sometimes included in Corbett's record as a *bona fide* competitive meeting, rather than a glorified exhibition, and one supposes that had Courtney managed to slip over a lucky one and knock the champion out he would have had a very strong claim to the world's heavyweight title. But he had been chosen with great care. Peter Courtney's one claim to fame was that he participated in the first-ever fight film. His earlier career as a boxer is shrouded in mystery. His later efforts, too, are consigned to limbo.

*   *   *

The next serious effort to film a fight of importance took place in February, 1896. It featured Bob Fitzsimmons and Peter Maher, and was one of the strangest affairs of its kind ever promoted. It is necessary to understand that while prize-fighting with the bare fists was definitely looked upon as illegal, and the comparatively new code of boxing with gloves was often winked at by the law, certain states in the American Union still frowned upon any kind of pugilistic combat. The Governor of Texas at that time, particularly, did his best to discourage any type of fist-fighting in his state, and it has always been something of a mystery why Dan Stewart, an experienced promoter, elected to stage the Fitzsimmons-Maher contest in territory where he must have known he would encounter difficulties.

Stewart arrived in the somewhat lawless border town of Langtry, Texas, on the date the contest was scheduled to be fought. With him were several hundred sports who had come to witness the meeting. But Texas Rangers, State Marshals, and even soldiers met them at the station, determined that no breach of the peace should take place in that particular town. But the authorities had reckoned without one 'Judge' Roy Bean, a notorious figure of the day who was the virtual king of that community, and who had, in fact, named the little town in honour of the famous beauty, Lily Langtry, whom he greatly admired. Bean was doing his best to see that the fight *did* take place, and he had made certain provisions. He led all concerned out of the town, right out of the United States, quite literally, into the gorge of the Rio Grande, and so into Mexico.

Almost on the very bed of the river an arena had been pitched. A canvas enclosure surrounded a boxing ring, and $20 was demanded from each prospective onlooker present. But a fair number of the fans decided that they would be able to see the fight just as well from the top of the gorge, from either the Mexican or the United States side. Many hundred spectators lined the high banks of the Rio Grande, and there was little need for the services of the famous Bat Masterson, who was armed with a gun and his reputation as Dodge City Marshal, to prevent possible gate-crashers at the entrance of the canvas enclosure. In fact, no more than one hundred and eighty-two people paid to go inside. The rest gained a perfectly good view of the ring for nothing, but when the fight began there was not much to see. It was all over in less than two minutes.

This occasion marked the first attempt to take moving pictures of a *bona fide* big fight between two good men. The Corbett-Courtney meeting had been a foregone conclusion as regards the result, and the fight had taken place in a studio. Here it was hoped that a film would be made under more serious and genuine conditions, but two things went to prevent it. Firstly, the day was overcast, and in those days it needed sun, and plenty of it, before successful pictures could be taken in the open air. Secondly, Fitzsimmons was out for a quick victory, and he scored it. The picture people had refused to pay him for the part he was to take in the movie, or rather, they didn't feel that the mere principals warranted payment. Fitzsimmons, like a good professional, was annoyed. 'All right,' he said. 'If there's no money there'll be no pictures.' He set out with the intention of making the bout so short that the film would be worthless.

The brief fight was practically all Fitzsimmons, but Maher did score one punch, which drew blood. After that the New Zealander went in, felt the Irishman out with a few long-range leads and then, as Maher struck out with a powerful left, Fitzsimmons neatly side-stepped it and loosed a hard right uppercut to the jaw. Peter Maher went down and was counted out. The official time for this fight was ninety-five seconds, and it constituted a new record for brevity in a heavyweight contest at that time.

Eight days later, Fitzsimmons and Maher were induced to box a 'no decision' bout of three rounds in New York for the benefit of the moving-picture people. They had registered nothing worth showing at Langtry, what with the weather conditions and Fitzsimmons's haste, but they desperately wanted a fight of some sort to exhibit to an interested public. This time Fitzsimmons demanded $10,000, plus fifty per cent of all profits, and he got it! This gives some idea of the attraction of fight films even in 1896.

It was Fitzsimmons's summary handling of Maher which was primarily responsible for inducing James J. Corbett to return to the ring after a long lay-off. Although he was the undefeated champion he had found that to capitalise on his reputation with stage work was far more to his taste and equally rewarding. He disliked Bob Fitzsimmons intensely, and had persistently ignored his challenges. He had even gone so far as to announce his retirement from boxing, and had nominated Peter Maher as his successor and the new 'champion'. Now his pride was hurt, and he came back in order to put the freakish New Zealander in his place.

The outcome, of course, is very well known. After outboxing his opponent for fourteen rounds, as well as giving him a pretty bad beating, Corbett was surprisingly knocked out by what became known as 'the solar plexus punch'. Coming out of a clinch, Fitzsimmons caught his man with a light blow to the jaw, then suddenly shifted his feet. He was in close, and for a fraction of a second Corbett's body was exposed. With everything he had, Fitzsimmons shot home a tremendous left to the stomach. It caught Corbett beautifully, and he dropped to his knees.

Fully conscious, and perfectly aware of everything that was happening, but in terrible pain, Corbett was unable to pull himself to his feet. At the count of eight he made a desperate clutch at the ropes as he tried to climb erect, but he missed them and fell flat on his face. Fitzsimmons was the new champion.

The defeated Corbett always claimed that the blow which beat him was a wild swing from nowhere, which Fitzsimmons sent in without any pre-arranged campaign or plan, while that punch has actually gone down in pugilistic history as the 'solar plexus blow' : a carefully-prepared delivery to the nerve centre just below the breast-bone, and one which Fitzsimmons had been intending to score all along at the second the opportunity presented itself. There is no doubt that the punch *did* land on the solar plexus, for it temporarily paralysed Corbett from the waist down and rendered him helpless and beaten while he retained full consciousness. The probable explanation is that the new champion, an illiterate man, had never heard of the solar plexus until he hit it and then read about it in the papers, but he had certainly been waiting for the opportunity to perform a quick shift with his feet and then sink in a knock-out punch to the 'wind', or the 'bread basket', as he more than likely termed the spot. In fact, in a statement after the affair he did say: 'I ... came in with a left-hand shift on his wind.' It was a manoeuvre he had used before to good effect.

Corbett was heart-broken over his defeat, and his manager, Bill Brady, had a hard job getting him to try and forget the knock-out and to think about luring Fitzsimmons into the ring again. But inducing the new champion to face Corbett a second time was a difficult matter.

Brady's method of attempting to force the winner into a return contest was a clever campaign with the film of the fight, which he first projected at the New York Academy with a running commentary of his own. His object was to prove that Fitzsimmons had been down for at least thirteen seconds in the sixth round – one in which the challenger had taken a particularly bad battering. In order to make the public believe this Brady had instructed the projectionist to slow the pictures down when Fitzsimmons hit the canvas. Counting normally to the audience as the referee's flickering arm waved up and down slowly, he managed to reach thirteen by the time the filmed count had reached nine and Fitzsimmons got up.

But unfortunately for Brady, the timekeeper sat in that audience, and he happened to be William Muldoon, as honest and as explosive a man as ever lived.

'That's a lie!' he roared from the gloom of the auditorium. Cinematography was in its infancy, and Muldoon knew very little about it, but he knew that the onlookers and himself were being tricked, even if he didn't know exactly how. But he kicked up sufficient of a fuss to cause Bill Brady considerable embarrassment. Corbett's manager was obliged to abandon his scheme very quickly.

The idea of hitting upon the long-count angle with the film to discredit Fitzsimmons, rather than upon any claims of a foul punch – which would have shown up in the film – is proof enough that neither Corbett nor his mentor really believed that the challenger really deserved disqualification that day, although they had raised a big enough squawk in that direction at the time. Jim Corbett, partly responsible for pioneering the first filmed fight, and having thrived handsomely from it, soon discovered that this new form of news entertainment was a double-edged sword.

Bob Fitzsimmons won the world's championship fairly, after having taken an awful beating, and perhaps the only thing that can be held against him is his stubborn refusal ever to meet Corbett within the ropes again.

Anyone who has consistently watched televised wrestling cannot have failed to notice how all the best and most spectacular holds are made to the advantage of the main camera covering the bout. It is not always so, by any means, as can be realised by attending a wrestling tournament where no cameras of any sort are in evidence. On such occasions there are four sides of the ring claiming equal entertainment, and an individual watcher will find that a 'live' viewing of a wrestling match is about a quarter as absorbing as a televised one.

Ring performers are no less human than stage or screen ones, or, for that matter, ordinary citizens not normally in the public eye. The consciousness of a camera lens pointed in one's direction appears to have an almost universal hypnotic effect. How often have you seen otherwise undemonstrative men waving or mugging in the crowd whenever a camera zooms down into a close-up of a corner-kick at a football match, or when John Rickman sums up the chances of the various horses at a race meeting? How often have you watched the impromptu televised street interview, and been distracted by the oh-so-nonchalant passer-by edging into frame in the background?

In 1922 Georges Carpentier, light-heavyweight champion of the world, signed to defend his laurels in opposition to one Battling Siki, a Senegalese Negro fighter who was not of the first class, shall we say?

Siki was one of the most flamboyant and colourful characters in the history of boxing. But apart from a couple of fights his record hardly bears investigation. I would not go so far as to say that both were fixed, but the first was a ghastly mistake, with a result quite unanticipated and financially embarrassing for many, and the second was a foregone conclusion from the moment of its inception.

According to all reports, Siki was a savage from the Senegalese jungles. He was more or less 'adopted' by a French actress on the strength of his remarkable sexual prowess, and was re-christened Louis Phal. In Britain, this might read as a perfectly respectable European name. But roughly translated, it means something like 'Joe the Cock'.

When he departed from his protectress and later took to fighting for a living in France, Belgium and Holland, he did pretty well against inferior opposition, and reverted to his childhood name of Siki. His career did not start in earnest until shortly after the First World War.

Now, in a lifetime of interest in this particular sphere of endeavour I have developed a retentive memory for the names of pugilists who have got anywhere at all in their chosen profession, and I can quite honestly say that up to a fateful day in September, 1922, Battling Siki had not faced more than three or four men who had any pretensions at all to a reputation. These were René Devos, a fair-to-middling French middleweight, Tom Berry, who later went on to win the British cruiserweight title, Harry Reeve, who had held that same honour years before in 1916, and Marcel Nilles, a man whose main claim to remembrance is that his name crops up – nearly always on the losing side, and by a knock-out – in the records of several other better-known fighters.

Battling Siki, on achievement, was nowhere in the running for a shot at the world's title when, in the summer of 1922, he was matched for that singular opportunity. At the time, very few people had ever heard of him. He was a hand-picked lemon chosen to make sport for a Parisian holiday.

Georges Carpentier was, at this period, undoubtedly the foremost heavyweight in Europe, and the greatest attraction. Admittedly slightly tarnished by having succumbed to Dempsey the year before, you had to go back to 1914 to find anyone else who had been able to stand up to him. He did not bother to train seriously for this first defence of his light-heavyweight title. He looked upon the contest as a glorified exhibition and an opportunity to display his talents before the camera.

Indeed, if you have been fortunate enough to see the film of this fight, you will have noticed that during the early rounds Carpentier was less concerned with defeating Siki than in so manoeuvring his opponent as to show himself in either full face or profile to the magic lens. He was so far in advance of Siki, pugilistically, that it is obvious that he was merely prolonging matters in order to enhance the value of the film which would shortly be shown in the cinemas of the world.

The champion did take time out from his posturing to whip over that famous right-hander which had humbled so many opponents, and it dropped Siki to the canvas but did not knock him out. Had Carpentier been more concerned with finishing the fight and less with showing himself to good advantage on film he could have terminated matters within the next few seconds. But he let the cringing and crouching Siki off the hook, and it was the greatest mistake he made in his life.

The Senegalese recovered, and I think it is quite possible that it occurred to him that he had taken the best that the great Carpentier could deal out and had come through the ordeal. At any rate, he was now no longer the sacrificial lamb awaiting the inevitable slaughter. He had an entirely new confidence, and he threw one over at a moment when Carpentier's attention was largely on the cameraman. It caught the champion beautifully, and floored him ingloriously.

Those who saw this contest from the close proximity of the ringside have said that from that moment Battling Siki reverted to the savagery of his youth and childhood. This is not evident from the film, which was shot from some distance, but it is clearly obvious that he now had the upper hand and was fighting with a ferocity he had never displayed before. Siki proceeded to give the untrained Carpentier one of the most merciless beatings ever seen in the boxing ring.

The French boxer, for all his vanity, his much-publicised matinée-idol charm and his Grecian profile, was still a hardened professional pug, and no quitter. He took the hiding of his life, and the spectators watched the almost berserk Siki transform him from the handsome, confident hero to a battered, bruised and bleeding hulk who was practically unrecognisable.

The end came in the sixth round, when Carpentier tottered to the ropes, took a murderous swipe to the jaw, and fell completely beaten. But as he fell, both his and Siki's legs became entangled, and the Negro wrenched himself loose and moved away. The beaten man lay flat on his back, with one leg, half-paralysed, stuck high in the air.

At the ringside there was pandemonium. Most of the onlookers, with the fickleness of all fight crowds since time began, now screamed their adulation of the underdog who had triumphed. Other factions, those heavily-committed betting boys, Carpentier's retinue, and the small hierarchy involved in pugilistic politics, jumped at the thin straw of safety and clutched it firmly. The upshot was that Siki was disqualified for tripping!

Immediately this announcement was made, the infuriated crowd made it quite obvious that they were prepared to pull the Buffalo Stadium to pieces in protest, and this whole, remarkable event marks one of the very few occasions when a referee's decision was overruled and reversed. While Carpentier was carried from the ring, literally more dead than alive, a hasty conference took place. In less than half an hour Siki was announced the new light-heavyweight champion of the world by a knock-out.

The film was shown all over Europe, and made a great deal of money. Siki, who had never been particularly affluent until this time, now became as ostentatious as only a man with his child-like brain could be. The most popular story of his brief days in the limelight revolves about his strutting the Paris boulevards with a lion cub on a leash. How pitifully naïve and unaware both he and his advisers were is shown by his agreeing to box Mike McTigue, an Irishman, in Dublin on St Patrick's Day, with the title at stake! Since the Black and Tan 'troubles' were at their height, with bombs exploding in the street, much must be said for Siki's blind courage as well as his stupidity. He lost the fight and his championship.

His pugilistic invasion of the United States was a failure. Apart from being quite undisciplined, he was never really a great fighter, and he came to a violent and premature end when he was found face down in the gutter of New York's Hell's Kitchen with a bullet in his back.

19 Southpaws

Of all the many unlovely things that have disgraced the boxing ring, none is more unlovely than the southpaw. For the benefit of the uninitiated, a southpaw is a left-handed fighter whose natural inclination is to face up to an opponent with his right fist and right foot foremost. Any heavy guns he might carry are usually associated with his left.

Henry Cooper, himself a southpaw *manqué,* came to subscribe to the widely-held belief that all 'wrong way round' boxers should be drowned at birth. This opinion, of course, is held because he had to meet one or two of them during his career, and they are awkward and difficult men to box. I have sparred with a few myself, in my younger days, and it is not at all nice. In fact, as far as I am concerned, boxing a southpaw is only about one degree less unpleasant than having to watch one.

Now, while no man can help being left-handed, and all the sympathy in the world should be extended to him for being, in all senses of the work, *gauche,* and in having to face all the petty frustrations encountered in a predominantly right-handed world, he is not at all attractive to watch in the ring. Whenever I am obliged to do so, I experience with my eyes something akin to that feeling that strikes my ears and teeth when 'an idiot child runs wild with a ball-point pen on a piece of slate'.

Anyone with the slightest aesthetic sense in regard to the art of boxing must dislike southpaws. I imagine that they cause considerable turbulence in other sports, too. Personally, I hate watching left-handed lawn tennis players or table tennis players. I can just about stand them in baseball and cricket, although I am irked when a right-handed batsman scores a single and the whole field has to be adjusted to cope with the southpaw who was at the opposite end. I wouldn't mind this so much if cricketing ethics didn't demand that under no circumstances, unless the ball is actually in play, should Kipling's 'flannelled fools' break into a trot. In soccer, however, by the very nature of the game, the left-footed winger is a positive boon and the provider of great aesthetic pleasure.

But I abhor the southpaw fighter. For some reason he is indigenous among the lighter men, and particularly in the amateur ranks. Many a simon-pure tournament has been quite spoiled for me by a preponderance of members of this breed. Happily, very few of them get very far when they elect to face more serious opposition among professionals. Happier still, they are practically non-starters among the big men. There have been very few left-handed heavyweight national champions, and no southpaw heavyweight world champions at all. In fact, off-hand, I can't think of any big man of this nature who ever posed a serious threat in first-class opposition.

20   Ring Oddities – III

Primo Carnera was an amiable and somewhat bovine pituitary specimen from a peasant community in northern Italy. He is, perhaps, the most pathetic example of the jetsam left by professional boxing's seamier citizens : those buccaneers and pirates of ruthless financial exploitation.

He stood nearly six-and-a-half feet tall, and he weighed something between seventeen and eighteen stone. He was built like the proverbial barn-door. Muscled like the Hercules of Praxitiles, he had the blind courage of the bull whose insignia he used to wear on the left leg of his fighting trunks. Unfortunately, he was also as docile as that same bull when surrounded by steers : steers who, in this particular case, also had the propensities of sharks.

Primo was possessed of a long-gummed and short-toothed, Grock-like grin, and a huge prognathous jaw. Some of the most educated and lethal fists of the nineteen-thirties bounced off that chin and china. They dumped him on to his broad backside and shoulders many, many a time, but none could keep him there. His guts and gluttony for punishment were both his glory and his undoing. His career as a fighter lasted roughly for ten years : he started with nothing, was built up to become champion of the world and earned fortunes for his owners, and he ended half-paralysed, once again with nothing.

An itinerant French pug named Paul Journée found him in a travelling circus. Carnera was working as a strong man and odd-jobber at the time. He would probably have had a happier life and a longer one had he never listened to the blandishments of the old fighter who told him of the riches and adulation awaiting him within and beyond the purlieus of the magical roped square.

The facts are these : Primo Carnera couldn't fight then, and he never could later. By dogged persistence on the part of coaches and trainers the fundamentals of the art of boxing *were* eventually instilled into him, much in the same way as a performing elephant learns to do its tricks, and he *did* eventually become quite a text-book stylist, going through all the motions he had been taught. But as a strictly manufactured boxer he was quite unable to adapt himself when the going got rough. Yet the image projected of him in the press was of an enormous, man-killing fighting bull, absolutely invincible and indestructible. He was never that. He couldn't take a really hard blow on the jaw without folding, although to give him his due he always unfolded immediately and wobbled erect to face further battering. More important, he was never able to punch his full weight, or anything like it. Strong enough to lift an opponent bodily and throw him back over his shoulder, he could nevertheless only half-punch and half-push a smaller adversary about the ring.

I well remember his début in London in 1929. The publicity and ballyhoo have never been equalled. He was reputed to stand nearly seven feet high and weigh twenty stone. The papers depicted his enormous paw covering a hand of bananas, and went on to tell how he devoured those same bananas as a preliminary snack before tackling the huge meal of spaghetti and ravioli which awaited him. He was photographed with both arms outstretched, and with his diminutive manager, Leon Sée, standing beneath one arm, with Sée's head not even touching Carnera's armpit. There was all this sort of thing, and much more. Small wonder that he packed the

Albert Hall when he faced his first English opponent, a luckless third-rater named Jack Stanley.

The sacrificial lamb did not stay very long. Carnera push-punched him to the canvas in less than a single round. I think it quite possible that the new phenomenon might have been fed quite a few more similar push-overs here had not Britain been graced, at that time, by a remarkable young American heavyweight by the name of Young Stribling.

A short digression is necessary here. Stribling was a full-time professional who had been fighting two or three times a month, quite literally, for many years. He was managed by his parents, show-business people who believed that the end justified the means. Their sights were on the big stuff : a world's title and the fortune that goes with it. Young Stribling was one of the two or three contenders among those on the short list for a title fight, but meanwhile there were groceries to be paid for. I betray no professional secrets or information not already common knowledge when I say that a great many of Stribling's barnstorming knock-out victories throughout the various towns and states of America were at the expense of the same opponent, under a variety of different names. The Striblings deliberately hoodwinked the public to gain their daily bread, and were open to propositions.

Young Stribling, although under six feet and less than fourteen stone, but nevertheless in world's championship class, boxed Primo Carnera, a highly-publicised novice, on two occasions in Europe, and my opinion is that these fights stink like month-old kippers.

Carnera's manager, admittedly none too sophisticated in matters of the ring, *must* have known that his fledgeling charge, with all his bulk, was not yet ready for a man of Stribling's vast experience in an honest fight. Yet, as I say, this pair met twice. The first time, in London, the American was disqualified for a low blow. The second time, in Paris, the Italian was ruled out for hitting after the bell had ended the round.

If I am hopelessly wrong, and am maligning all those concerned, then the results only prove all the more strongly that Carnera was nowhere near ready for first-class opposition. In their London meeting, Stribling, a blown-up light-heavyweight, actually floored the vast Carnera with relative ease. The Ameri-

135

can always claimed that when the fallen giant scrambled to his feet he was quite berserk, and that the subsequent low blow was deliberate and calculated as the only means open to avoid himself from being torn to pieces! In the Paris fight, Carnera was so unschooled and undisciplined as to ignore the bell and continue boxing after the round had ended.

Early in 1930, Leon Sée invaded the United States with a great fanfare of trumpets and much beating of the big drum. There now began the most blatant and phoney build-up of any man in boxing history. Naturally, the wolves moved in. Carnera was such a potentially valuable property that an insignificant European like Leon Sée could not be relied upon to guide his fortunes without help. Sée was gently leant upon, and was induced to sell a piece of his property to those who had more advantageous connections in the profession. It was put to him as diplomatically as possible: without an 'in' he was 'out'.

The Carnera circus barnstormed its way throughout the States in a series of pre-arranged fights against hand-picked opponents, twice a month on average. In March alone, Carnera boxed six times. Most of these affairs terminated in the first or second round, almost always with the opposition lying flat on the canvas in complete relaxation, listening to the count.

These extravaganzas served a dual purpose. They were widely publicised, and portrayed Carnera as an unbeatable knock-out specialist. They also imbued a wonderful feeling of confidence in the unfortunate Italian dupe. He really thought that he was knocking over these formidable men like so many ninepins. It must be remembered that at this time he could hardly speak English at all, and never went anywhere alone.

Only two of his adversaries during this first fantastic American year were not exactly happy about the arrangements. Both, as it happened, were coloured. The first was George Godfrey, a big Negro who had, for years, been in championship class, but who had been denied an even break because of his complexion. He lost the fight, as he had to, but lost it by sinking a blow well below the belt and incapacitating Carnera. He thus retained both his reputation and his honour. The second was

Bombo Chevalier. He agreed to take a tumble, for being an under-privileged journeyman-pro who must have encountered similar things before, he was well aware that the build-up was part and parcel of the apprenticeship of a good and young prospect. But the contest had not progressed very far before Chevalier came to realise that he was streets ahead of this supposed man-killer he was facing as regards sheer skill, and he saw a short cut to fame and fortune. He tried the old double-cross. It took the combined efforts of Primo Carnera, Chevalier's own seconds, who tried to blind him with chemicals on the towel between rounds, and even the referee, before he was beaten. Bombo Chevalier signed the death warrant to his own career, of course, but he informed a discerning section of the public what was going on in an article that was published in a national magazine.

However, as I have pointed out elsewhere, the general public's capacity for self-deception has no limits. While the sporting fraternity now had a pretty good idea of what was happening, the average man in the street continued to believe that Carnera was a real fire-eater. With great avidity he followed the barn-storming jaunt across the continent, while the Ambling Alp, as the good-natured Italian giant had been dubbed by the reporters, pushed and shoved his carefully-selected opponents to the canvas.

There is no knowing how long this business might have continued, had not the Carnera circus pitched its tents in Boston that October. Those responsible for matching their bread-winner elected to pair him with a native son named Jim Maloney. Now admittedly, Maloney was past his best. Indeed, he was rapidly approaching the end of his career, but only a year or two previously had been one of the best two or three heavyweights in the world. His undoing had been a so-called 'glass chin': he could not absorb heavy percussion to the jaw. It was felt by those guiding Carnera that their man was ready to take on a man of Maloney's class and beat him in fair fight. Looking back, and knowing the facts, this seems quite daft now. Jim Maloney was by far the best man Carnera had ever met, with the possible exceptions of Stribling and Godfrey. The big fellow's own managers must have come to believe the extravagant publicity their man had been receiving.

What happened was that Carnera couldn't hurt Maloney, and the Boston man's experience enabled him to outpoint his opponent comfortably over ten rounds.

This brought the Italian's first American trip to an abrupt end. He was shipped across the Atlantic to Barcelona, where he boxed another 'name' opponent, old Paolino Uzcudun, the Basque : a very tough guy indeed. The fight took place in the local bull-ring. Carnera got the decision : he also nearly got lynched. It was an uninspiring bout, but sufficiently closely-contested to cause the Spanish crowd to riot, when the verdict went against their man. In all fairness, I should add that at this particular stage in that country's history it took very little to arouse two or three thousand gathered together to begin breaking up everything in sight.

Just before Christmas, Carnera came to London again, but his mentors were careful enough to pit him with home-grown material not likely to cause too much trouble. Reggie Meen was big enough, and well-known enough, to make the prospective contest look something like a real match, but although he went on to win the British title eventually, he was a long way from being among the first flight of pugilists.

This bout gave locals like myself an opportunity to see how far, if at all, Primo Carnera had progressed. I recall that before a packed auditorium, he entered the ring with the gimmick of stepping *over* the top rope, rather than ducking under it. His waltz versus Meen showed us little, beyond acquainting us with the knowledge that he was far too hefty for anyone but a heavyweight of the very first class to make an impression upon him. Meen was a fifteen-stoner, and willing enough, and I don't think Carnera hurt him in the slightest. But the bigger man just shoved and wrestled his opponent off his feet. It was like a middleweight cuffing a game featherweight around the ring. The whole thing was so one-sided and ridiculous that the referee stopped it in the second round. No bones were broken, no blood was seen, and nobody got hurt.

The following year Carnera went back to the States. His first adversary was Jim Maloney, who had exposed his deficiences five months earlier. This time the verdict was reversed.

Either Maloney had regressed amazingly, or he had been made to see the error of his ways in outboxing so valuable a property. The most charitable thing to say is that he was finished as a fighter. He retired after one or two further unfortunate excursions.

Big Primo, now with his confidence fully restored, embarked upon a second barnstorming tour against inferior opposition. He scored six successive knock-outs between June and August, 1931, and these affairs totalled less than eleven rounds.

It has always been a mystery to me why his American managers, purportedly shrewd men who intended to nurse their charge into the really big money, should feed him such a diet of blatant set-ups and then throw him a really tough bone to chew on. Leon Sée had done it first with Stribling back in 1929. The Americans did it again with Maloney in 1930. Now, in 1931, they moved into New York and did it with, of all people, Jack Sharkey! This character, mark you, was the leading challenger for the heavyweight championship of the world. He had knocked out Maloney in five rounds and had outpointed Stribling over ten. He not only gave the relatively inexperienced Carnera a boxing lesson and a severe trouncing, but was the first man to expose the giant's inability to take a really good blow to the jaw. He sent Primo flat on to his back and did everything but keep him there. Incidentally, he also went on to win the world's title in his very next fight.

So now began yet another build-up for the unfortunate and docile Carnera, to regain his lost prestige. This time it took place, for the most part, in the various capitals of Europe, and to be fair about it, one must admit that he was facing pretty fair 'class' opposition. But now there were few of those quick knock-out victories, and twice he was extended to the full limit of ten rounds. Then he was paired with that experienced veteran, the coloured Larry Gains, and once more the well-laid plans came unstuck. Gains beat him well on points at the White City.

Back went the whole ménage to the United States, intent upon erasing this blot from the escutcheon. But by this time the American boxing public was growing just a little tired of the whole Carnera business. It had been clearly proved that he was no world-beater. In fact, it seemed very much as though

139

he was well on the way out when a big fellow from Jersey City, named Stanley Poreda, gave him a neat boxing lesson. This fight put Poreda up among the title contenders but, ironically, it was practically the last worthwhile exhibition he ever gave. The following year he was knocked out in four successive fights and drifted into limbo. The more cynical have suggested that this was his reward for being so ill-advised as to humble the potential gold-mine named Primo Carnera. There is certainly no doubt that he plummetted from being one of the foremost championship challengers to complete obscurity in a matter of about twelve months.

By this time, Carnera's image had altered considerably. He had developed into a fairly good rote-type boxer, but he was a dull and plodding performer. The customers still paid to see him, but they came in their droves now not with the expectation of seeing him clobber a luckless adversary to the canvas, but with the hope that somehow, somewhere, sometime, one of these opponents would club *him* into oblivion.

This silly symphony reached its crescendo in the year 1933. Now, it should be clearly understood that up to this time Carnera had defeated in decisive fashion *not one fighter* who might be termed of championship class. All his victories, the push-and-shove brawls of brief duration and the extended, pedestrian, ten-round slow waltzes, had been at the expense of trial-horses, selling-platers, 'has-beens' and, in some cases, 'never-wassers'. The only 'name' men he had beaten in fights which I believe would bear investigation were Jim Maloney, Paolino Uzcudun, and King Levinsky. This last-named gentleman was a rather squat but willing performer with a round-house swipe which could have pole-axed Carnera had it ever landed. But to his detriment he usually sent a telegram ahead of it every time, informing his opponent that it was on its way. Even the cumbersome Carnera had no difficulty in brushing it aside.

In 1933 the champion of the world was the rather unpopular Jack Sharkey, of Boston. He had won the title the previous year with a somewhat controversial decision over the German, Max Schmeling. Madison Square Garden, to whom he was under contract, was a profit-making company which was looking about for a money-spinning challenger, and that year had produced a pretty poor crop. Big Primo, although he had done nothing sensational, looked like the best bet. Another man in the running was a young Bostonian named Ernie Schaaf, who had jumped to the fore by knocking out Stanley Poreda. But there was a certain difficulty about Schaaf : he came from the same stable as Sharkey, so to speak. They were both managed by the same man. Further, Jack Sharkey owned half his contract, came from the same town, was also an ex-sailor, and had, indeed, been something of a tutor to him. A match between this pair would smack very much of keeping the whole thing inside the family.

When Schaaf and Carnera were coupled in an elimination match to decide Jack Sharkey's next title opponent, the whole thing looked very fishy to some people of a cynical disposition. It looked, and smelt, decidedly fishier when the news leaked out that Carnera had already been signed by Madison Square Garden to fight a championship bout, well before the issue with Schaaf had been settled. The whole thing stank to high heaven during their contest. Schaaf was listless and unimpressive : he fought throughout in a half-crouch, and he took quite a buffeting about the head from his enormous opponent. Angry voices were raised long before the thirteenth round, when Ernie Schaaf slipped gently to the canvas and appeared to be feigning unconsciousness. The crowd knew quite well, by this time, that Carnera couldn't punch.

Schaaf was carried from the ring, still apparently oblivious, to the accompaniment of a chorus of boos and cries of 'Fake !' A section of the audience was still quite unconvinced when it was announced that Schaaf had been taken to hospital in a coma. When he died a few days later, without having regained full consciousness, some of the doubters changed their tune. Was this Primo Carnera literally a man-killer, after all ? Had Ernie Schaaf's last fight really been on the level ?

After a full enquiry, Carnera was absolved from all blame, although I, for one, would very much like to know what poor old Primo thought, and felt, at this stage in his career. If we have ever been informed, in public print, I must have missed it.

It eventually transpired that Schaaf had never really been quite the same man since the previous August, when he had taken a very bad battering about the head from a young Californian named Max Baer. I am more than inclined to accept this, but it doesn't say much for whoever pronounced Schaaf fit for the Carnera bout. Schaaf had, it would appear, been living on borrowed time ever since he faced Max Baer.

And so Primo Carnera was steered into a match for the championship of the world, still without a solitary, really impressive victory over a first-class man behind him. His fight versus Sharkey at Madison Square Garden's enormous Long Island Bowl ranks as probably the most dubious affair ever waged for the coveted heavyweight title. It ended abruptly in the sixth round, when Sharkey backed to the ropes, took a short, right uppercut to the chin and fell flat on his face, to be counted out. Certain experts who sat at the ringside said that they did not see the final punch. One very well-known journalist dryly reported that Sharkey succumbed to 'an uppercut to the lower lip'. It was an unsatisfactory conclusion, to say the least.

Now that Carnera was champion of the world, it was proclaimed far and wide that he would hold the title for years, that there was nobody at all on the horizon who stood the slightest chance of beating him. His owners quickly capitalised by whisking him to the land of his birth and showing him to his own countrymen in Rome against a carefully-selected antagonist. Before a capacity crowd, and as the high spot of a tournament mounted by Benito Mussolini to the glory of Fascist Italy, Carnera plodded his way to a dull fifteen-round points victory over the somewhat elderly Paolino Uzcudun. It was said that, under such circumstances, the Spaniard would have had to knock Carnera cold to even get a draw! This time there was no riot: the native son was cheered to the echo. But the fact remains that this bout has been all but forgotten, outside of Italy.

The big fellow also defended his title at Miami early in 1934 against a man who must have been the least dangerous heavyweight of any prominence his mentors could find. Tommy Loughran was a clever and crafty veteran who had been boxing since 1919, and who had won the light-heavyweight title as far back as 1927! Weighing only a little over the poundage for that division, he had been mixing things with the bigger men in an effort to box his way to the major and more lucrative championship. It is ironical that when at last he was given the chance he had wanted for so long, Loughran, the smallest of all the heavyweights of the time, should be asked to face the biggest. He had forgotten more about the art of boxing than Carnera would ever know, but he could get nowhere near the champion. Primo spent a large part of the contest treading on Loughran's toes, and using his beef to shove the smaller man around. Yet for all his great weight advantage, the Italian could not hurt his opponent or even knock him down.

The only fighter who looked as though he might give Carnera something of a scrap was Max Baer, a swashbuckling clown of a man who took nothing seriously, but who carried a punch so powerful that it was almost literally lethal. Frankie Campbell had died after being knocked out by Baer, and Ernie Schaaf, of course, had also come to a sad end some months after fighting him. Baer was just approaching his best at this time, and was the logical challenger for Carnera's laurels. But those in charge of the big fellow's fortunes were doing their best to stall. Money had to be made, but in the least hazardous manner possible. There now occurred an incident which must be unique in the history of the sport.

Max Baer, good-looking, popular and sheer 'box-office', was signed to star in an important Hollywood boxing movie, to be called *The Prizefighter and the Lady,* opposite Myrna Loy, and supported by Walter Huston and Otto Kruger. Plenty of money was being scattered about in its production. Someone had the brilliant idea of engaging Primo Carnera as Baer's adversary in the climactic celluloid punch-up, with Jack Dempsey, no less, to act as the referee. Louis Soresi and Bill Duffy, who were in charge of the champion's finances, had no objections to this at all, or to the considerable thousands of dollars they were to be paid. But they did not like the idea of their property being humbled and shown to be beaten in the mock film-fight, although the script naturally called for such an ending. After considerable wrangling, Carnera's 'honour' was saved by the script being altered to depict a compromising draw, with Baer taking a bad beating early on and then coming back with a grandstand finish to equalise matters.

The film was shot successfully and did very well wherever it was shown. Everyone was happy, but none more happy than

143

Max Baer, for he discovered during the filmed sparring sessions with the champion that in an honest-to-goodness scrap with the big fellow he could win with ease! He also established an enormous psychological advantage : brash, quick-witted and worldly-wise, he kidded the pathetic and unsophisticated Carnera unmercifully throughout their sessions at the studios.

The time arrived when the reluctant Carnera camp could no longer stave off Baer's demands for a fight. The upshot was that when the pair met that summer in a real-life battle for the championship, there resulted the most farcical, sensational and one-sided title match this world has ever seen. Max Baer almost slaughtered the unfortunate and bemused Italian. Clowning to the delirious onlookers, and fighting in short, serious spurts, he floored the giant with powerful swings to the jaw no fewer than eleven times in the ten rounds the affair lasted. On several occasions the powerful Carnera pulled Baer to the canvas with him as he reeled and stumbled before that murderous onslaught. His courage was little short of heroic. Boxing throughout in the sterotyped manner in which he had been taught, he had no answer to the attack to which he was subjected. Floored again and again, he did not know enough to stay down and seek the respite of the referee's count. Time after time he wobbled erect almost immediately to face further furious punishment. His corner was in an uproar. His chief second, a business man, was too ignorant in ring matters to instruct his principal wisely. The one-sided farce ended when the battered Carnera, limping from a broken bone in an ankle which had buckled under him as he had fallen early in the fight, signalled to the referee that he could not go on.

Now that the Carnera bubble had been well and truly pricked, the best thing that could have happened would have been for his managers to allow him to slip quietly into retirement and to return home to Italy and enjoy the fruits of his labours. But that would not have been good business. I have no doubt at all that Primo Carnera himself was now sick of the ring, but he had no alternative but to obey the orders of his masters. He had so many managers, trainers, advisers and hangers-on, all taking a share of his earnings, that very little was left over for the pathetic dupe who was forced to take the knocks. He was bound and tied, contractually, for as long as they wished.

It was quite obvious that Carnera could never regain the title – at least, so long as Max Baer ruled the roost – but there was always the possibility of a return fight. The fans would turn out in their thousands with the prospect of seeing another slaughter of the same type as that first encounter.

So poor Primo continued. They shipped him to South America, where he was still something of a novelty, and for a few months they made hay while the sun shone in a tour through Argentina, Uruguay and Brazil. Then, in the summer of 1935, a new phenomenon arrived in New York : Joe Louis.

I think few will disagree with my statement that Joe Louis was among the greatest half dozen fighting men who ever lived. Indeed, some people would name him the greatest. Certainly, as a combination of clever boxer, two-fisted fighter and destructive puncher, the world has never seen his like. In 1935 he was a slim youth of twenty years, and had been a professional for just one year. Already his fame had spread across the world after a score or so of sensational wins in the Detroit and Chicago districts, but he had not yet been seen in New York. Hardened fight experts who had seen so many phenomena come and go declined to throw themselves overboard for this latest until he had shown himself in the Big Apple. He had to meet a 'name', and to prove his worth. What better name was there for his first big trial than Primo Carnera?

Those of the post-war generation, if they remember Joe Louis, recall him as a pretty hefty and thick-set veteran who had been at the top for so long that he had become a living legend. In 1935, when he shuffled out of his corner for his first big test he was a stripling almost dwarfed by the enormous ex-champion. He was well aware that Carnera possessed sufficient muscular strength and reach advantage to cuff him about considerably and to shove him off balance if he were allowed to do so, and Louis therefore boxed to a preconceived plan. At the outset he eschewed all close-quarter mixing and attempts to score one of those early dramatic wins which had brought his name before the public. He inched forward in his unique flat-footed stance and stuck out a consistent hard left jab to his opponent's body.

Louis boxed in this way for five rounds. When they came out for the sixth, Carnera's ribs were bruised and sore, and he had absorbed quite a pasting about the stomach. It was now, when once again the moon-faced young Negro began to throw those long, weakening punches to the mid-section, that the Italian's guard wavered and dropped. For the first time in the contest his gloves were held low, and his head exposed.

Suddenly, with a speed and power that few of the onlookers had dreamed he possessed, the young man whipped over a terrible right-hander which caught Carnera full on the mouth. It was the hardest punch he had ever received, and was probably one of the hardest that Louis ever delivered.

It smashed Carnera to the canvas. There, with his senses reeling and his legs like rubber, the hapless giant wobbled to his knees, his eyes rolling and his mouth a crimson gash. Not one man in the crowd would have blamed him had he elected to stay down for the count from that terrible blow, but Carnera forced himself erect and turned to face Joe Louis. He walked into one of the fiercest and most merciless attacks ever seen in an American ring.

The next few seconds stamped the Negro then and there as a fighter of world championship class, but they also stamped Carnera, with all his faults and deficiences, as a man of the highest courage. He really took a terrible beating, and as fast as he was smashed to his knees he staggered upright again and faced more punishment. Eventually the whole thing became so one-sided that the referee stopped it to save Carnera from permanent injury.

Eliminated from all future consideration as a title challenger, Carnera was now matched with opponents just shy of the front rank. People still paid to see him, but always with the high expectation of witnessing yet another Jack-the-Giant-Killer episode. They were rewarded in March, 1936, at Philadelphia. Here, one Leroy 'Tiger' Haynes, a thick-set Negro, not only battered him into submission in three rounds, but left him paralysed down one side and a hospital case. The big fellow recovered sufficiently to fight a return contest, but only succeeded in prolonging his agony until the ninth round.

Primo Carnera was now a worthless property. He was jettisoned, ruthlessly and irrevocably. He returned to Europe, broken in health and in spirit, no wealthier than when he had first started boxing there nearly ten years earlier.

He fought just twice more. One Tony Duneglio outpointed him in Paris, and Josef Zupan brought his career to an end in a couple of rounds in Budapest, late in 1937.

I have read elsewhere that the Primo Carnera story had a happy ending. It is certainly a fact that after the war was over he was talked into going back to the United States as a wrestler, and that this time he made sure that he held on to the considerable money he was able to make, and I suppose that this is where the aforementioned happy ending lies. But Primo Carnera didn't have all that pleasant a time after he gave up fighting with his fists. During the war, in the Italian army, he had a pretty rough deal, and on one occasion I remember reading that he had been killed in action. He wasn't, of course, but he was very badly wounded.

In the late Forties, sentiment alone led me to make a pilgrimage to Harringay Arena, where he was billed to wrestle one of his earlier conquerors, Larry Gains. This character was another of those pugilistic unfortunates who had not held a very firm grasp on his earlier riches and had now been obliged to join the ranks of the grunters and groaners for subsistence. It was a pathetic spectacle. There were no gimmicks this time, I noticed, like stepping over the top rope : Carnera entered that ring conventionally and with obvious boredom at the whole rigmarole. When the announcer introduced him and insisted on that now worn-out old spiel about his enormous, and vastly exaggerated proportions, Carnera openly sneered and turned his back with a derisive gesture. This wasn't part of the pre-fight corner histrionics we have come to accept from wrestlers : Primo was weary of the whole reiterative malarkey. He had heard so much of it, so many times before.

When he doffed his robe, I was surprised to see the extent of one of his war wounds. It was just over his right kidney. He had a hole there you could have put your fist into.

The wrestling match, of course, was utterly ridiculous. Larry

Gains, who, as a boxer, had made Carnera look like a novice, stood no chance at all when he came to grips with his old opponent. If the whole business was *bona fide,* Gains did remarkably well to last as long as he did.

Carnera died a few years later. The effects of those batterings in the boxing ring, together with the aftermath of his service during the war, eventually caught up with him.

'The bigger they are, the harder they fall.' It is an old pugilistic adage. In 1947, Budd Schulberg wrote a remarkable novel, clearly based on Carnera's career, and he used the last half of that old maxim for his title. He also quoted two lines from John Milton's *Samson Agonistes,* which serve admirably as an epitaph for Primo Carnera :

> I sorrow'd at his captive state, but minded
> Not to be absent at that spectacle.

21   Apocryphal – III

Shortly after Max Baer's disastrous fight versus Joe Louis I read an anecdote which amused me very much at the time. It was the first occasion I had encountered it.

The story had it that after the opening round Baer tottered back to his corner and slumped on to his stool. Jack Dempsey, his friend and second, said to him : 'You're doing fine, Max. He's hardly touched you.'

Baer took heart at this encouragement and went out for the second round. He weathered this one successfully, and when he returned to his stool at the bell, Dempsey informed him : 'Great, Max! He hasn't laid a glove on you!'

The third round was pretty hectic. It ended with Max Baer battered and bleeding on the canvas. Only the bell saved him from a knock-out. Back in his corner, as his seconds worked over him desperately, Jack Dempsey's words had the same familiar ring. 'Marvellous, Max. Keep it up. He's hardly hit you once.'

Baer turned wearily to his comforter and said : 'Then for Christ's sake keep your eye on that referee, Jack, 'cos someone out there's giving me a hell of a licking !'

I have heard this story a dozen times since, and always with fresh actors in the principal roles. As I say, I learned of it first with Baer, Louis and Dempsey playing the parts. It was published in a national daily newspaper and was written by one of the foremost boxing reporters of the day, who ought to have known better. My guess is that a variation of the tale was probably told with great glee after the Sullivan-Corbett fight, or even before that.

22   One on His Own

One of the most publicised boxers who ever lived was Gene Tunney. But at the same time he is, in my opinion, probably the most underrated fighter of all time. He is remembered as a good, but not a great champion. Fight fans tend to think of him as a light-hitting but clever boxer who took the world's heavyweight title – and for the first time ever on a points decision, by the way – from a living legend called Jack Dempsey, who was past his best. Their inevitable return contest produced the most controversial incident in the annals of pugilism, the famous Long Count, and Gene Tunney comes out of it second best, although he actually won the bout. After that, Tunney fought just once more, defending his title in what he called 'the most satisfactory contest of my career'. But from the points of view of the promoter and most of the cash customers it was a ghastly failure. He then quietly retired.

This retirement, virtually in 1928, set boxing into something of a slump. It was 1930 before a new heavyweight champion was crowned, and *he* won his title on a disqualification, sitting on the floor of the ring and claiming a foul. The early Thirties produced much activity, and considerable change of tenure as far as the coveted heavyweight championship is concerned.

Most of the holders are now considered as being rather small potatoes. It was not until 1937, with Joe Louis ruling the roost, that boxing's chroniclers and historians – and its money-making impresarios, of course – found things back the way they liked them to be. Gene Tunney is usually blamed as being the responsible party for the slump. He should have stayed, apparently, until he got knocked silly.

Newspaper reporters, as a race, don't like Gene Tunney. This isn't really surprising. He could have done *their* job, more or less, as well as he did his own, and the idea of this hurts. But such a statement as this needs some clarification, and a couple of illustrations.

Imagine a training camp. The fighter is working hard for a big contest. In comes a widely-read sports reporter: a man worth the greatest consideration. He watches every move and notes each apparent fault or deviation. He asks questions, of manager, trainer, and boxer. He is not particularly bothered about the answers he receives; whatever he is told can be paraphrased later on in the office to suit his waiting millions of readers. Quite often he has made up his mind about the angle his story is going to take long before he ever went to the training camp and did his interviewing and watching. He is known as a boxing expert. Even those he is writing about often tend to take as gospel the opinions he voices, although occasionally they suspect that he might be talking through the top of his hat.

Now imagine a newspaper office. Experienced journalists are working hard on their stories. In comes an obvious plug-ugly, barely worth their consideration. He asks questions, looks over their copy, points out errors in grammatical constructions, and observes in laughing superiority their faults in syntax. He then returns to his camp and relates it all to his trainer and sparring partners. They all have a good giggle.

The first of these illustrations happens very often. The second occurs very, very seldom.

Now, the personality of a prominent boxer only becomes known to the general public from whatever may be written about him by reporters. The pieces they type are naturally flavoured by their predilections. Professional writers, used to visiting various pugs at their particular camps, are also used to weaving a readable story out of a virtual nothing. They were somewhat taken aback, to put it mildly, when interviewing Gene Tunney. They found that here was a man who was not only able to answer their questions quite coherently, but one who rather uncomfortably seemed to put them in the position of the pupil asking the teacher, rather than that of the teacher asking the pupil.

These reporters, perhaps rather naturally, resented Tunney's literacy. Their pride was hurt. It was very much the same as if a visiting writer had been invited to put the gloves on with a champion, just for a laugh, and had then proceeded to thrash the experienced professional pugilist.

It is not surprising that many of the writers, when they came to report on Tunney, and to compose 'profiles' of the man, tended to paint him rather unflatteringly, and to sneer.

Gene Tunney was not normally a spectacular fighter. Although he won consistently throughout his early years he never chalked up dramatic one-round and two-round knock-outs as, say, Dempsey had done on his way to the top. In addition, he suffered from brittle hands, and the word got around that he wasn't much of a puncher. But it should never be forgotten that the bout which eventually won him a chance at Dempsey's title was a masterly twelve-round knock-out at the expense of Tom Gibbons. This formidable character Dempsey had earlier failed to drop for a count in fifteen! Gibbons had also scored no fewer than thirty-eight knock-out victories himself in his last forty-six contests. Now, I have seen a great many fights 'live', and a great many more on film and television, but I have never in my life seen two more superbly-timed and exe-cuted right-handers than those with which Gene Tunney knocked out Tom Gibbons.

Tunney started off as a slim and gangling light-heavyweight who boxed just for the fun of it, in New York City, with his youthful friends and acquaintances. He was a volunteer in the U.S. Marines when the Americans entered the First World War in 1917. He went overseas, but he saw no active service. As an alternative to the endless drills and guard duties he chose to box for his unit, without seriously considering the ring as a possible profession. Nowadays the serving ranker, lacking the ability to do the same thing, would refer to such a colleague as a 'jock-strap'. Tunney was pretty good, and when he won the light-heavyweight championship of the American Expeditionary Force in Paris, the seeds of an idea were sown.

Taking stock of himself, with demobilisation ahead, and no definite job to return to when he got to the United States, Tunney quite simply decided that the one profession for which he was suited, and in which he could most quickly make a fortune, was boxing. Jack Dempsey had just won the world's heavyweight championship. Gene Tunney, an unknown amateur light-heavyweight, made up his mind to build himself into a full heavyweight and take Dempsey's title. He confided in very few people, and this was just as well. Most of those he did tell had a quiet little laugh about it when Tunney wasn't around.

Hundreds of fighters go into this business, of course, secretly believing that somehow, and at some time, they will reach the top. It's a good thing for boxing that they do. But very, very few go about it in the manner of Gene Tunney. He decided to take no chances at all: he would never face another man in the ring until he, Tunney, had decided that he was ready for this particular opponent.

In the whole of his career Tunney made only one mistake in this direction. In 1922 he thought he was good enough to beat Harry Greb, and for fifteen rounds he took one of the worst beatings ever seen in an American ring. His nose was broken by almost the very first punch Greb threw, and he bled profusely from deep cuts throughout the whole of the contest. Tunney showed amazing courage in staying erect until the final bell, but collapsed almost immediately afterwards.

The American light-heavyweight championship was at stake in this gory contest, and Tunney was extremely disappointed to lose this, his first title, only a few months after he had won it from Battling Levinsky. But within a year he boxed his way back to prominence, challenged Harry Greb, and completely reversed things by outpointing his opponent over fifteen rounds and regaining the championship. A few months later he did the job again, beating Greb by an even wider margin.

This pair boxed on two further occasions, and each time Tunney showed increasing superiority over Harry Greb. After their last meeting, Greb frankly and graciously admitted that Tunney was his master, and from that moment forward was as convinced as Gene himself that the great Jack Dempsey's days as heavyweight champion were numbered.

Tunney's complete mastery of Harry Greb, the only man who ever gained a decision over him, is all the more remarkable considering that Greb is remembered as one of the greatest middleweights and light-heavyweights who ever put up his fists. Rough, tough, and wildly unorthodox, he nevertheless had that spark of fistic genius in him. There is a story to the effect that he once gave Jack Dempsey quite a pasting in a gymnasium sparring bout. It may well be apocryphal: certainly I have never encountered anyone, in print or otherwise, able to quote chapter and verse, but there is no denying that Dempsey and his advisers steered well clear of Harry Greb in serious public conflict.

In six or seven years of almost continual ring activity, training, and the study of potential opponents, Gene Tunney met and defeated, among others, Battling Levinsky, Tommy Loughran, Harry Greb, four times, Georges Carpentier, Tom Gibbons and Johnny Risko. From the lanky light-heavyweight who had started in 1919 he developed into a real big 'un of almost fourteen stone.

After he knocked out Gibbons, Tunney became the logical contender for Dempsey's title, but it should be remembered that the champion had earlier engaged in two million-dollar extravaganzas versus colourful men who had been deliberately built into 'foreign menaces': the French Carpentier and the Argentinian Luis Firpo, big-punching and exciting figures who had looked as if they might topple the great Dempsey. When promoter Tex Rickard eventually signed Tunney to meet Dempsey in 1926 he did not do so from choice. There just happened to be no better money-spinner about.

The two previous million-dollar affairs had attracted the vast attendances they had done, to a large extent, because of the uncertainty of the outcome: the possibility, embellished by skilful press agents and publicity, that Jack Dempsey was going to take a hiding. This time it was impossible to build up the champion's opponent as being the fire-eating man-killer, like Firpo, or the lightning-fast and deadly-striking matinée idol, like Carpentier.

This time the crowd which paid a million dollars to see the great Jack Dempsey box Gene Tunney at Philadelphia in 1926 stumped up its cash in the expectancy of seeing the champion smash into insensibility an unpopular and presumptuous challenger. Dempsey had not fought seriously for three years : during that time his name had become a legend and he was looked upon as invincible. Tunney had been plodding along successfully, but for the most part unspectacularly. He always won, but he seldom impressed. And, of course, the newspaper reporters, who didn't like him very much, betrayed their wishful thoughts through their finger-tips at their typewriters.

That the whole world viewed him as being hopelessly the underdog was not lost upon Gene Tunney. It did not bother him at all. It probably bothered him just a little when he discovered that his own manager had bet against him to lose, but not to the extent of undermining his confidence in himself.

Tunney amazed the whole world, and incidentally gained a considerable psychological advantage over his prospective opponent, by travelling to the scene of the fight from his camp in a plane. Today, a hop through the clouds of a few hundred miles would appear commonplace : fighters regularly journey the three thousand miles across the Atlantic by air and would consider it irksome to have to do the trip by sea. But in 1926 things were very different. If a present-day American challenger were to sign to box a title bout in London, took off in a rocket from Cape Kennedy, and splashed down in the Serpentine for the rendezvous, it could not cause much more of a sensation, by comparison.

It has often been said that Jack Dempsey was not at his best for this particular fight. He was certainly ring-rusty. Innumerable sparring exhibitions and even intensive training-camp preparation can never equal the occasion of a tough fight under serious conditions against a first-class opponent. In addition, Dempsey had been plagued by law-suits and domestic worries. On the other hand, Tunney's plane flight had proved to be something of a boomerang. He was air-sick for most of the journey. While his close associates were impressed by the fact that he retired to a hotel room and calmly slept until it was time to leave for the stadium, this was not because of his ice-cold confidence and lack of nerves, but because he felt more dead than alive.

All true followers of boxing know that Gene Tunney won this contest, and the championship of the world, by methodically outboxing and outpointing Dempsey over ten rather unexciting rounds in what some people have called a steady drizzle and others have called a downpour. Certainly it rained throughout the whole contest, soaking the onlookers, and this did nothing to lighten the gloom that settled over the stadium as the 120,000 spectators watched the end of a legend. But, as Christopher Morley once said, 'You can't have gods without *Goetterdaemmerung.*'

Something should be said here of the great Jack Dempsey, who, for all his fame, is really nothing more than a respected name to many sportingly-inclined youngsters nowadays. He had a unique style, never satisfactorily imitated by anyone else. He boxed high up on his toes, but his body was usually bent in a half-crouch, with his chin tucked well down on to his chest and with his eyes peering up at his opponent through beetle brows. He continually bobbed and weaved: that is, the movement of his head drew a sort of figure-eight on its side as he moved in towards his man. He was very fast, and was extraordinarily difficult to hit with a solid blow. He himself was a devastating puncher with either fist as he danced in, light as a fairy on those spindly shanks, coming up out of his crouch with short hooks.

In 1926, when he faced Tunney, he had fought only about three bouts in the past ten years which had gone longer than half-a-dozen rounds, and during this period he had waged something approaching fifty contests – so-called 'exhibitions' included, in which he never pulled his punches. For this reason his popular image portrayed him as a cave-man type of slugger relying on brute force, but the fact is that he was a far better boxer than most people have given him credit for being.

He probably made the biggest mistake of his career in believing, with untold millions of others, that the unspectacular Gene Tunney did not present really serious opposition. Yet, after the fight was over, commentators found it difficult to imagine any other conclusion than the one which occurred. Tunney, for all his lack of colour, was a superlative ring-artist : he had outboxed the cleverest of his contemporaries, and these, as I have mentioned earlier, included Carpentier, Gibbons and Loughran. By dictating this fight from start to finish and seldom allowing Dempsey to get near enough to do any serious damage, he built up an impressive lead on points in the early rounds, closed both of his opponent's eyes with punishing long-range jabs and, in racing parlance, won the fight 'going away'.

When Gene Tunney accepted the promoter's offer to meet Jack Dempsey for the heavyweight championship of the world he knew, as certainly as a man can know anything, that he would win. Dempsey may not have been quite the same man he had been three or four years earlier, but this makes no difference. If Tunney had thought he could not beat the Dempsey of 1926 he would have declined the fight. Cold, calculating and dispassionate, a highly-intelligent man of business as well as being a magnificent athlete, he was, truly, one on his own.

23 The Battle of the Long Count

The summer of 1927 saw the most publicised and discussed boxing match ever staged. For months before it took place the world's newspapers devoted many pages to it, and when it was over, but far from forgotten, the clamour raged for many more months. Today, that fight is still a topic of conversation wherever boxing fans gather, but apart from one short incident, about which the controversy has flamed, the bout lacked many of the thrills associated with other famous title contests.

It all began when Jack Dempsey, who had announced his

retirement after losing his heavyweight championship to Gene Tunney, decided to try and win back his laurels. Tex Rickard, the promoter, desperately wanted him to return, since a second fight between the two would mean yet another fortune for all concerned, but for a time Dempsey, the old Manassa Mauler, was adamant, and stayed in retirement at his home in California. But as the months passed, and the bitterness and the despondency of his defeat at Philadelphia wore off, the battle urge and the lure of the ring came back. The old champion took up light training to see if he could work himself back into something like fighting trim. Very soon he found that he was feeling quite fit, and with a totally different outlook from that which he had had prior to the Tunney fight in 1926. He told Rickard that he would have a shot at a come-back, and immediately the promoter began to arrange things.

At this time the man who held pride of place as challenger to Gene Tunney was a young ex-sailor from Boston, named Jack Sharkey. Tex Rickard paired him with Dempsey in an elimination bout, and announced that the winner would be the man to face Tunney in September, 1927, in the fight of the year.

Just how popular Dempsey had now become, and just how great a fighter the fans believed him to be was proved by the number of people who turned out to see him and the amount of money they paid. This was the first million-dollar bout in which no championship was actually involved. The fans flocked to see the return of the legendary Manassa Mauler, and for the first time in his career they were behind him almost solidly, all hoping that he would blast his way back to a contest with Tunney and topple the aloof ex-Marine from his pedestal. 75,000 people paid a total of $1,083,530 for the privilege of seeing this fight.

Dempsey did not disappoint them. Sharkey, the younger man, took most of the points in the early rounds, but by the sixth his opponent began to take the initiative with spirited charges and attacks to the body. Dempsey opened the seventh in the same manner, still boring away at the mid-section. It was at this point that Jack Sharkey's unstable temperament, which later led him to become so disliked, first began to show. Instead of fighting back, as Dempsey would have done had he been in the other's place, Sharkey backed away and claimed that the blows were low. Next, a stiff dig in the solar plexus almost knocked him down, and then he did a most ridiculous thing: he dropped his hands and turned to the referee.

Dempsey didn't falter. He immediately shot a left-hook to the unprotected jaw and Sharkey fell flat on to his face, knocked out.

Of course, there was plenty of criticism from some directions about the manner in which Dempsey won this fight, but he was well within his rights, since the rules demand that a boxer must protect himself at all times. In addition, his image had never revealed him as a gentleman-boxer type who handled his opponents with kid-gloves, so to speak. He had always been known as a bit of a rough 'un, and his newly-found popularity suffered not one bit. This fight gave Jack Dempsey the opportunity of meeting Gene Tunney in a return contest for boxing's greatest prize.

Tex Rickard appointed Leo P. Flynn, one of his business associates and the former matchmaker at Madison Square Garden, as Dempsey's manager. It was done with the former champion's consent, of course, but as Tunney himself noted, this somewhat unusual move showed how close the promoter and his best money-spinning fighter were in those days. Shortly afterwards, Flynn employed Bill Duffy, an astute but somewhat unethical gentleman straight out of a Damon Runyon story, to help him. News of Dempsey's connection with Duffy, together with Flynn's apparent position as liaison officer, looked very fishy to some people. It caused the inevitable rumours to be circulated: this coming fight would not be on the level. Most common of these rumours was the one which suggested that Jack Dempsey had deliberately lost his championship the year before in order to make an enormous sum of money by betting against himself, and that now, with the odds against him in the second fight, he would be backing himself to win, and would win easily. Tunney, too, was supposed to be a party to this arrangement, having made his own share in the Philadelphia contest. The rumour circulated so freely that in certain quarters it actually came to be regarded as a fact.

When it was announced that Chicago was to be the scene of the fight, even more rumours spread. Chicago in 1927 was probably the most corrupt city on earth. The gangster and racketeer, Al Capone, was virtually its king, and many of the police and government officials were on his pay-roll. He was a heavy gambler, and he had bet $50,000 that Dempsey would win. When this became known it was considered that the Manassa Mauler *must* be a sure thing for the coming fight. After all, All Capone wouldn't bet all that money on a fight that wasn't fixed.

Normally, the odds might have been on Tunney to repeat his Philadelphia triumph. As things were, with the rumours of Dempsey's certain victory, plus the doubts and the many speculations about what actually *would* happen, the betting gradually changed to even money. It was a toss-up – anybody's fight.

Gene Tunney did everything possible to ensure that he was not double-crossed during the contest. His primary concern was the choice of an impartial referee. He was not interested in holding the title if he could not retain it honestly, but he wanted an official who would show no bias towards either man.

As the day for the fight grew nearer, so something of a panic began to spread among certain elements in Chicago. So much money was being wagered on this affair that it seemed almost positive that the sure-thing boys were on to something good. They intended to make certain that the referee, whoever he was, would be a crook : someone who would give Dempsey the decision whatever happened. Tex Rickard, his associates, and even prominent Chicago business men who were anxious to avoid a scandal, were desperate as they tried to get to the bottom of the plot. Finally, the Illinois State Boxing Commission took things over and announced – as it should have done long before – that the referee would be an honest and capable man who could not be got at, and whose identity would not be known until the last moment.

Then another rumour got around that Tunney would be

taking a dive in the seventh round. As it happened, the seventh round was the session which made this fight so well-remembered, and during its course many thousands of hearts almost stopped beating with uncertainty and excitement.

Both boxers trained for the battle of their lives. Jack Dempsey had sustained an injury to his eye in the Sharkey fight, but otherwise he was perfectly fit. Telling of his approach to this contest, he says :

> I thought I had a fifty-fifty chance of defeating Tunney in our return engagement at Chicago. I knew I was in far better shape than I had been at Philadelphia the year before, and that even then he hadn't knocked me out in ten rounds. My legs were stronger than they had been. My wind was better. I had more endurance. Best of all, I had under my belt the hard and successful fight against Sharkey. Against these things there was the cut over my eye, which had bothered me a good deal. I didn't want, anyway toward the end of my ring career, to risk permanent damage to my eyesight. Victory wouldn't be worth that much. I already had all the money I'd ever need to live on, and even my fans wouldn't ask me to lose an eye to regain the title.*

Tunney had an accident during his training which was not disclosed until well after the contest had been fought, and which has been described both by Tunney himself and by Eddie Eagan, the former amateur champion, who was helping the ex-Marine in his preparations. It appears that during a sparring bout with a fighter named Frank Muskie, Tunney ran into a crack from his partner's head which knocked him out on his feet. Tunney completely lost consciousness but floored his opponent. He then took on Eddie Eagan, who was a close friend of his, and gave him a very vicious beating. Afterwards he took off the gloves, and until the following morning he was sullen and quiet. When he awoke the next day he could remember nothing of what had occurred.

* Jack Dempsey. *Round by Round* (Chapman & Hall, 1941).

As I lay in this state of returning consciousness, I became awfully frightened. Gradually my name came to me. That I was a pugilist soon followed, and then the thought of being champion – impossible – unbelievable. I must have had a long dream. Slowly came the realisation that I had not been dreaming. I rose and asked guarded questions. I wanted to know all about the events of the day before. For three days I could not recall the names of my most intimate acquaintances. I had to stop training and did not leave my cabin, except to eat or take a short walk. On these occasions all seemed queer. I was unable to orient myself. The sensation I had was as though hot water had been poured through a hole in my skull and flowed down over the brain to my eyes, leaving a hot film.*

Tunney confided to Eagan that something was wrong with him, but they told nobody else. Gradually the clot of blood, if that was what it was, passed from his brain, and Tunney returned to normal. But it was this accident which, although leaving no permanent damage, led this champion to retire from boxing much earlier than he might have done. For weeks he was haunted by the possibility of becoming punch-drunk and ending his days in the pathetic condition so many other unfortunates of the ring had reached.

It was in this state of mind that Gene Tunney entered the final period of preparation for his contest with one of the most deadly hitters and punishing fighters the sport had known. What would the champion's attitude to further boxing have been back in 1922 had his fight with Harry Greb left him not with a horribly cut face, a broken nose and the loss of much blood, but with a temporary concussion or clot on the brain? Would Tunney have stuck to his resolve to win the title, or would he have abandoned his quest then and there?

The second Tunney-Dempsey fight was fixed for ten rounds, the limit for contests held in Illinois, as in Pennsylvania. 22 September was the date, almost a year to the day after their first meeting, and the prices of seats were raised for the great

* *A Man Must Fight.*

event. As Rickard had anticipated, the largest boxing gate of all time resulted. The official attendance was 104,943 persons, nearly 16,000 less than the crowd at Philadelphia, but the receipts totalled $2,658,660 – a fantastic figure. So many reporters were accommodated round the ring – men from all over the world – that the first row of so-called ringside seats for the pay customers was a considerable distance from the scene of combat. At the outer rim of the gigantic stadium, Soldier's Field, the ring must have appeared very tiny, and any far-off spectator who did not carry field-glasses could not have seen many details of the bout. It was probably for this reason that Tunney wore a pair of brilliantly white shorts, while Dempsey was arrayed in dark ones. Identifying the contestants by the colours they wore was just about the only way many of the onlookers could tell the boxers apart.

The betting was even when the men entered the ring, but there may have been some frantic last-minute backing of Dempsey when the referee ducked between the ropes. His identity had been kept secret until the last moment, and his appearance was surprising to many ringsiders. He was Dave Barry, a man whose integrity was unquestionable, but some people were aware that he disliked Jimmy Bronson, who was closely connected with Tunney. The champion himself had been rather afraid of Barry being selected. However, Dave Barry showed complete impartiality throughout the fight and handled a most ticklish situation with a clear and steady mind and according to the letter of the state boxing rules.

Before the men went into action, a detailed conversation took place in the centre of the ring between Dempsey, Tunney and Barry. Both boxers had been given a book of the rules to study, and both knew just what was allowed and what was not. Barry explained that in the event of a knock-down occurring, the man who scored it was to retire to the farthest neutral corner. Both boxers agreed, and Barry further explained that unless the man *did* go to the corner the count would not be started until he complied. Dempsey has since stated that this stipulation did not appear in the printed rules; Tunney has said that the referee explained the rule verbally and quite lucidly there in the centre of the ring, as reported. Either Dempsey was not listening very carefully or Tunney invented the whole

162

conversation, which is unlikely. A further explanation is that Dempsey, in the heat of battle, lost his head. He certainly had the contest as good as won when he refused to abide by that rule and go to a neutral corner.

The early rounds were almost a repetition of those of the first fight, except that Tunney did not land a hard right in the opening round this time, as he had done in their first match. He certainly tried to, as the film of the contest shows. He took the aggressive immediately, but being over-anxious to end the bout quickly, he confessed : 'I threw and missed more rights than I ordinarily would have in twenty fights.'

Dempsey crouched and weaved, occasionally attacking vigorously, but again Tunney scored the more points and looked as though he might repeat his earlier victory in the same manner : boxing at long range and taking few chances now that he saw that he could not land an early knock-out punch. By the end of the fourth round Tunney had cut both of Dempsey's eyes and had landed one heavy right which troubled the old Mauler.

Dempsey did everything he could to rattle the champion and tempt him to come in and have a fight, even to the extent of landing rabbit-punches in the clinches. Although both the rabbit-punch and the kidney-punch were foul blows and had been agreed upon as such, Dempsey knew that the referee would think twice about disqualifying him for these infringements in a bout with so much at stake. A great deal of latitude is allowed in a world's championship fight, and Dempsey was aware of it only too well. Despite protests from Tunney's corner, Dave Barry did nothing to stop those chops on the back of the neck. The recipient did not appear to be inconvenienced by them, and he was certainly not going to allow their use to goad him into dropping his arms and complaining as Sharkey had done. Neither was he going to lose his temper and rush in at Dempsey to retaliate. In a word, he was completely the master of the situation.

The Manassa Mauler showed something of his old form in the fifth and sixth rounds, but he did little damage. Yet the bout was halfway through, and he had to do something spectacular soon or lose the fight. Tunney was winning by a mile and all he needed to do was to keep well out of danger and the decision was his. This knowledge led Jack Dempsey to come out for round seven with as near an approach to the fighter he had been in his heyday as was possible.

He countered a straight-left with a hard right to the jaw which sent his man hopping back. Tunney was more hurt by it than he knew, for Dempsey's next punch, an obvious left-swing which a man of the champion's ability should have picked off with ease, landed full on his jaw. It shook Tunney, and he backed to the ropes, which was something he had never done willingly before in the fight. Dempsey saw his opportunity and went in.

Tunney felt the ropes at his back, realised his danger, and came away from them quickly. He walked right on to a perfect left-hook, and his knees buckled. Then Dempsey let loose a barrage of punches which pounded Gene Tunney to the canvas. The champion was down, and for the first time in his life!

His back fell against the ropes, but the weight of his limp body caused him to slip sideways a little. He was sitting on the boards with a foolish look on his face, and he grasped the middle rope instinctively with his left glove and pulled himself up a trifle. Had the rope not been there it is highly probable that he would have fallen flat on his back, and the subsequent trend of events might have been very different.

Immediately Tunney was floored, the knock-down timekeeper began to count. Dempsey stood right over the fallen boxer as the crowd rose to its feet with a roar. Dave Barry jumped forward and waved Dempsey to the neutral corner, then looked towards the timekeeper to pick up the count from him. Dempsey, like a great sullen cat, sidled round Barry and stood close-by, in the nearest corner, his own, never taking his eyes off Tunney, who was sitting bewildered on the canvas.

Suddenly, Barry noticed Dempsey behind him and stopped counting. He pushed the fighter away and pointed across the ring.

'Go to the corner, Jack,' he said.

'I stay right here,' replied Dempsey. He grabbed the top rope with his right glove and still watched Tunney. All this time the seconds were passing, the timekeeper was steadily noting them, and the crowd was screaming for Barry to take up the count.

But the referee, in accordance with the rules, made no attempt to begin counting until Dempsey conformed with them. Finally, after what seemed an age, although it was actually only a few seconds, Dempsey heard the frantic yells of his retinue just below him, realised that he was penalising himself by not standing clear, and then shuffled right across the ring into the farthest neutral corner.

Only then did Barry turn once more to the fallen champion and begin the count all over again. By the time he had reached nine, Tunney had been on the floor for at least fourteen seconds. Some reports stated that he was down for nearer twenty seconds, but Leo P. Flynn has said that by the stop watch he carried Tunney had a respite of fourteen seconds. Being a member of the enemy camp, so to speak, it was in his interest to stretch things a little, but he was scrupulously honest about this. I happen to possess a copy of the film of the contest, which I have run many, many times, and at varying speeds, both forwards and in reverse. Taking the falls of Dave Barry's arm as being at one second intervals, Tunney was down for a little over fourteen. It is this period of time which has come to be accepted in this controversial event. The actual length of the champion's stay on the floor is not important. He was definitely down for more than the prescribed ten seconds which signify a knock-out; there is not the slightest doubt about that. What most of the shouting has been about since the occurrence is whether he could have arisen in ten seconds had Dempsey gone across the ring immediately.

Some people think that he could have got up: others say he couldn't. In giving his own version of the fight, Jack Dempsey did not actually say that he thought Tunney could not have beaten the count, but it is pretty safe to estimate that he did think so. As for Gene Tunney, he dealt with the happening thoroughly on more than one occasion, and he tells us that he could have arisen.

According to Tunney, he could have jumped up at any time after the count of four. He says that when he became conscious that he had been floored he looked straight at his corner, saw his seconds signalling him to stay down, and nodded. Then he heard the referee say 'Two.' Accepting fourteen as the number of seconds he was on the floor, that means that he became aware of his surroundings after he had been down for six, and would have heard Barry say 'Seven' under normal circumstances, and not 'Two'. Then, if he could have arisen any time after the count of four, as he says, ordinarily he could have got up after nine! That is leaving it pretty late, even for a man as unique as Gene Tunney. He may have thought he could have left the floor at that time, but it is extremely doubtful that he could have done. Trevor Wignall, who sat next to the timekeeper, and who had a perfect view of the fallen champion, has said :

> ... I was in the best possible position to estimate Tunney's state, and I am prepared to swear that for seven or eight seconds he was incapable of movement. I was only a few yards away from him and during these seconds he was either gazing dazedly at the canvas or, (apparently), straight into my face.*

When Tunney fully understood the position and knew that he had until the referee dropped his arm for the ninth time, he took full advantage of the respite allowed. The stunning effects of the rapid succession of blows which had knocked him down passed as quickly as those final seconds, and when Barry raised his arm to drop it for the tenth time, Gene Tunney got up.

Dempsey had been standing tensed and waiting in the angle of the ropes, ready to shoot out of the corner if Tunney arose, and now he hurled himself forward in the most desperate attack he had ever staged. Had Tunney elected to stand and fight back, or even had he leaned on the ropes and covered up, nothing could have saved him. He had beaten the count, he was conscious, and his legs felt all right, yes, but even the fittest of men cannot recover completely immediately from a barrage of punches such as he had received. His timing and co-ordination were still not quite as they should have been, and his head reeled. There was only one sensible thing to do, and he did it. He started going backwards, round and round the ring, never getting too close to the ropes or a corner to allow Dempsey to reach him. He took not the slightest notice

* Trevor Wignall. *Prides of the Fancy* (Nash & Grayson, 1928).

of the frantic screams of the thousands who yelled at him to stand his ground and fight. Tunney ignored the crowd completely and concentrated every nerve and muscle on the job in hand : that of keeping out of harm's way until the bell sounded, and avoiding that crushing punch which the scowling and murderous-looking Jack Dempsey was intent upon sending over.

Perhaps not one in a thousand boxers could have dodged and retreated successfully from such an attack for any length of time. Gene Tunney, improbable as it seems, eluded Dempsey completely, and therein lies his true greatness as a pugilist. He had foreseen some such occurrence as this many years before, and like the ring general he was, he had made ample provision for such an emergency. He reasoned that there were several alternatives of what he might do : he could fall into a clinch and hang on as best he could, he could attempt to take advantage of his opponent's anxiety to end the fight and so score a really telling blow himself, or he could retreat as fast as he was able. During the last seconds he was on the floor, Tunney discarded the clinch as a manoeuvre because of the inevitable rabbit-punch which Dempsey would try and which the champion knew would fell him again. He also discarded the gamble on launching a telling right-hander as Dempsey came in with an attempted finisher himself, on the grounds that the Mauler's punch would probably land effectively while his own would never reach the vulnerable point because of this particular opponent's habit of attacking with his chin on his chest. The best Tunney could hope for was to score on the brow or the cheek, and that was not good enough. There was only one thing for it, and that was to keep away. That Tunney finished the seventh round even stronger than Dempsey is proof enough that he fully succeeded in carrying out his plan.

A part of his unorthodox training always had been to run backwards as fast as possible. The result was that he could retreat quicker than many men could advance. Jack Dempsey chased him round that ring as fast as he could, but not once did he manage to score a single heavy blow. On the other hand, Tunney was able to shoot out some straight jabs as he went back which caught Dempsey coming in. A few of them were hard enough to slow the old Mauler's advance and make him think, but not one of them really hurt him.

Then, shortly before the bell, Dempsey suddenly ceased his futile chasing of the champion and paused. He lowered his head, stood firmly in the centre of the ring and beckoned Tunney to come in and fight. This grandstand gesture sent the already excited crowd almost delirious. Everyone was yelling enthusiastically for Dempsey now, and any fighter with a less calculating mind than Tunney might have responded to the invitation. Not so this one. He sensed that Dempsey had made the motion simply because he was now too tired to do any more chasing, but he was still dangerous. Tunney banked on one good dig which would tire his man even more. So, still backing away from a slowly-advancing opponent, he worked an opening for a smash to the heart. Then, as Dempsey came in with a sudden rush, Tunney stopped dead and went forward with a right-hander to the ribs.

Dempsey said that the punch was the hardest he ever took. 'It was not a question in mind of being knocked out – I thought I was going to die. I could not get my breath.' He took the full force of the punch as he was going in, and it doubled him up and almost sent him to the floor. Had Tunney been in a better condition himself to follow up that blow he might well have knocked Dempsey out just then. But he was not yet in a state to attempt to swap blows, and although that punch halted the ex-champion's forward rushes and caused *him* to go on the retreat, Tunney was now content to fiddle in safety until the bell rang. When it clanged to end the most controversial round in pugilistic history, Tunney was still moving round and trying to clear his head, while Dempsey was covering up and making no attempt to force matters. Of the two, the Manassa Mauler was the more badly hurt.

As the men sat in their corners during the interval between the seventh and eighth rounds, the crowd speculated wildly on what would happen in the three ensuing sessions. Tunney had won most of the early rounds on points, then Dempsey had scored the one knock-down in the seventh, had forced Tunney to back away for a full minute, and had then apparently tired and had made no further effort to score a knock-out. Most of the onlookers did not realise what power had been

168

behind the punch that Dempsey had taken, and it is improbable that the referee appreciated the damage it had caused. On the face of things, Dempsey had had all the better of round seven, and it was certain that he would force the pace during the remainder of the fight in order to try and duplicate his knock-down, or at least compel Tunney to take the defensive. The older man's superior aggressiveness might easily result in his catching the eyes of the officials and getting the verdict.

Tunney knew that he was ahead, but he also knew that apart from the one blow at the end of round seven, he had not shown to very good advantage during those hectic three minutes. To steer clear of trouble for rounds eight, nine and ten was one way of getting through the battle on his feet, but it would mean that Dempsey's inevitable grandstand finish might well win him the fight by a close decision. With this in mind, Tunney answered the bell for the eighth round with the knowledge that he had to do something pretty spectacular himself.

He accomplished it about halfway through the round. For a time he back-pedalled, leading Dempsey to believe that he was still groggy, or nervous that the knock-down would be repeated. He managed to score often enough with light jabs to the face delivered at arm's length, but they did little harm to Jack Dempsey, who still came on. The Manassa Mauler drove a tremendous right to the body which landed and sent Tunney hopping back, and then Dempsey came forward to follow it up. The champion stepped in quickly and clipped him on the jaw with a perfectly-executed right. It dropped Dempsey to his knees and dazed him. Dave Barry jumped forward to begin the count as Tunney started to walk away, but Dempsey was up almost before the referee had opened his mouth. Had there been less urgency about winning this fight, the old champion might have taken a rest and tried to shake off the effects of the blow, but time was short. Besides, a lengthy stay on the canvas would wipe out the advantage he had scored in the previous round. He staggered to his feet and charged in again, but that punch had done its work. From that moment forward there was no doubt about the winner. Dempsey still tried all he knew, but his legs were weakening, his wind was almost gone, and the swings he now began to deliver were often well wide of their target. Tunney began to force matters and took the round by a wide margin.

Rounds nine and ten were all Gene Tunney. He had completely recovered from the knockdown, he saw that Dempsey was in no condition to do much damage now, and therefore he went in with everything he had. He hit the failing old Mauler without a return. He cut Dempsey across the bridge of the nose, jabbed incessantly at his opponent's already split and swollen brows, and continued to pile up points. His punches were hard and accurate, but he could not score a direct blow to the point for a knock-out. Dempsey stuck it out like the true champion he had been and took an unmerciful hiding. The last round of the fight saw him growing weaker and wobblier with each succeeding second, while Tunney grew stronger and more sure of himself. He was boxing at the finish as though he could go on for another ten rounds, while Dempsey had the hardest of jobs in lasting through to the end on his feet. When the bell closed this historic contest, the verdict was so obvious that the reporters did not wait to hear it before informing their offices of the result.

When it was announced that the champion had successfully retained his title, the two boxers walked from their corners and shook hands in the centre of the ring. While a sentimental crowd booed the decision, Dempsey showed nothing to suggest that he disagreed. He was bitterly disappointed, of course, but he was a great sportsman. He knew that Tunney was his master. In his own words :

> There was no question about who had won. Tunney was credited with outscoring me in seven of the ten rounds, while even my most enthusiastic well-wishers couldn't score more than three for me.*

The official score-cards of the judges gave six rounds to Tunney, two rounds to Dempsey, and two even. On points, there was no room for disagreement, yet to this day thousands of fans insist that Jack Dempsey won by a knock-out in the seventh round and was robbed of the honour of becoming the

* *Round by Round.*

first man to regain the heavyweight championship of the world under Queensberry rules.

He was not robbed. He definitely scored a near knock-out, and he might well have won then and there, or at the very latest with one or two more punches, had he gone straight away to the neutral corner as the rule demanded. It is doubtful if Tunney could have arisen inside the bare ten seconds, but giving him the benefit of the doubt and assuming that he could have done so, it is even more doubtful that he could have retreated with the same success he had after the extra seconds on the canvas.

On paper, that famous second Tunney-Dempsey fight left the reigning champion in clear supremacy, but the long count had robbed him of a lot of the glory as far as the public was concerned. In fact, it was Jack Dempsey who was the hero of the day, and thousands believed that if the pair could be matched again the Manassa Mauler would be able to knock Tunney out. Tex Rickard saw the advisability of a third contest, and he lost no time in putting the idea up to the principals. Tunney was willing enough, but he stipulated that this time the contest would have to be over fifteen rounds. However, when Jack Dempsey was approached, his reply said everything there was to say, cryptic though it was in the telegram he sent to the promoter. 'Count me out, Tex,' he wired to Rickard. Those two fights had proved to one man's satisfaction, at least, that Gene Tunney was the better man.

24   Ring Oddities – IV

It is not a commonly-known fact that a former British Empire heavyweight champion was once managed by an impoverished young journalist and reporter who later became one of the most famous writers of his time. This was in Paris, back in the early nineteen-twenties. The one was an itinerant Canadian Negro : the other was an expatriate American.

During the time they were together neither man was particularly successful. Those who knew them both in Paris could
never have guessed how far each would go in his chosen profession. Of the two, of course, there is no doubt that the
manager went farther than the fighter. In literature, best-
sellerdom and universal acclaim might be termed the equivalent
of a world's championship.

Larry Gains, the boxer, never reached a world title : he never
even fought for that honour. But he did beat two men who
later attained that enviable height. In 1925 he knocked out
Max Schmeling in two rounds, on one of the very few occasions
the German was put down for the count, and in 1932 he outpointed Primo Carnera.

Gains was an accomplished journeyman who plied his trade
from Europe to Canada and the United States and then back
to Europe again. He reached the age of thirty before he really
clicked. He beat the British champion, Phil Scott, in two
rounds and, incidentally, ended that gentleman's career. Almost overnight he thus became something of a national
sporting hero in Britain, where he wasn't extremely well known.
He had confined most of his European activities to the continent.

This engaging and colourful personality arrived in the big
money when he was somewhat past his best as an athlete. This
did not deter him. Great Britain was not exactly bursting with
talent at the time, and Larry Gains made hay. For several
years he stood head and shoulders above any fighter in this
country.

More or less simultaneously with my awareness of this sleek,
minor phenomenon in our midst came my discovery of a young
and virile writer who was also just beginning to make a big
name for himself. Without knowing anything of their earlier
business relationship, I watched one start to rise to the greatest
heights and the other begin to fall.

The writer, whose style and choice of subject matter had
such an effect on impressionable young people of my age in
the late Twenties and early Thirties, seemed a very long way
away from a good-looking coloured pug named Larry Gains.
Yet I remember reading a wonderful novel of the 'lost generation' in Paris, and I read of a Negro boxer in this book, whom

I took to be a purely fictitious character. Nobody in that novel, of course, is wholly fictitious. Indeed, over the years, it has amused a great many people to identify the characters in the book with their real-life counterparts. The black-skinned boxer is certainly the fledgeling Larry Gains.

The author, if you have not already guessed it, is Ernest Hemingway. His book was called *Fiesta,* the original title of which, in America, was *The Sun Also Rises.* From the start of his career he saw himself as the potential champion of all word-slingers. He never had any doubt at all that he eventually became the undefeated title-holder. After writing *Across the River and Into the Trees,* in which, in my opinion, he lost his crown, he said : 'It is sort of fun to be fifty and feel you are going to defend the title again. I won it in the Twenties and defended it in the Thirties and Forties, and I don't mind at all defending it in the Fifties.'

Never particularly modest about his achievements in writing, he did admit that one old champion might have bested him. 'I started out very quiet and I beat Mr Turgenev. Then I trained hard and I beat Mr de Maupassant. I've fought two draws with Mr Stendhal, and I think I had an edge in the last one. But nobody's going to get me in any ring with Mr Tolstoy unless I'm crazy or I keep getting better.'

Old Larry Gains, well after he had retired, had a warming solace in that in his day he had beaten two erstwhile world champions. If he was proud of these achievements he had a right to be. I doubt if he ever boasted much about the penniless young poet and reporter who once handled his affairs, not particularly successfully, back in the early days in Paris. Yet Larry Gains had a unique distinction. He was the only fighter whose fortunes were guided by a man who was one day to win the Nobel Prize for literature.

25 The Ring and The Book

Bernard Shaw once wrote to the effect that two sure ways of attracting readers are to describe the murder of a child or to describe a fight. Well, as far as I am concerned, infanticide has never held any particular attractions, but I must admit to a weakness for the printed word dealing with fights – particularly boxing contests. For something like forty years I have devoured with great avidity the descriptions of many, many bouts of fisticuffs, some imaginary, but mostly real. During this time I suppose I have read almost every book about boxing of any real worth, as well as plenty of the others. The range is wide: from Pierce Egan's famous *Boxiana,* first published in 1812, right up to the latest 'autobiography', purportedly written by the current phenomenon of the ring.

Over the years there has been a steady stream of memoirs, reminiscences and life-stories, attributed to champions, managers, trainers and promoters. Some are better than others, but I have found very few of them quite unreadable. But I do not think I am betraying any secrets when I say that almost without exception these books were actually penned by professional writers. In fact, I would go so far as to say that probably only two books supposedly written by the boxers or their camp staff were actually set down without outside editorial aid. These two books are *A Man Must Fight* and *Arms and the Man.* I believe that both of these were written, unaided, by Gene Tunney. I concede that the several books of reminiscences bearing the names of impresarios like Charles B. Cochran and William A. Brady, highly literate men, might largely have been put together by those whose by-lines appear on the title-pages. The rest were written by experienced journalists and reporters.

This activity is known as 'ghost-writing', and it extends to the memoirs and confessions of footballers, cricketers, film stars, politicians, and, in fact, any persons in the public eye. Even more than a few authors have had ghost-writers, either when they are past it or too busy to meet all their commitments. I have had something to do with the job myself. It is a fascinating business, and bears certain rewards, apart from the financial ones. For instance, in my extreme youth I looked up to a particular champion, who had a great reputation as a two-fisted puncher. I wished like hell that I could fight as well as he could, and felt decidedly inferior to him. His affluence and success went to his head, and he was inclined to settle all arguments, with men *and* women, by a quick right-hander. Eventually he declined, both pecuniarily and physically. Many years later people read sentences and opinions which were mine and which they thought were his. Since I am only human, I confess that I now felt decidedly superior to my former hero, particularly since by this time he was only too glad of the few quid the use of his name an earlier reputation brought him.

On the other hand, ghost-writing carries with it its portion of gall. As a young man submitting unsolicited articles to a variety of sporting periodicals in an effort to establish myself as a writer on my particular sport, I naturally accumulated my fair share of rejection slips and seemingly unsaleable work. I was then approached by a gentleman who had quite a reputation in professional pugilism as an authority, and who also had a particular axe to grind. One or two international magazines were prepared to publish anything that bore his signature. For several years I supplied both this gentleman and the editors with material which I had hitherto been unable to sell under my own power. I simply substituted a new title-page to my type-scripts, appending another name instead of my own. Without exception, all these previously rejected articles were paid for, published and well-received.

My worst experience at ghost-writing was extremely humiliating. The 'name', who was on the spot, was asked to interview a contestant in a world's championship bout at his training camp. He, in turn, asked me to write his article for him, which I did. It was duly sent to the editor of the magazine who had commissioned it, who ghost-wrote the ghost-writer! Assuming that *my* work had been written by the person originally approached, he recast the article in its entirety. My job *must* have been bad. After that, I gave up this particular ghost.

* * *

As long as you are prepared to accept the fact that your pugilistic hero didn't actually sit down and write the words you are reading, there are some fascinating books in existence to while away your leisure hours. Almost every great champion has, at some time or another, produced an autobiography. A few have been gracious enough to add the words 'as told to' on their title-pages, with the name of the person who did the job for them in smaller type under their own. A few others will allow a foreword or preface, signed by either a well-known journalist or somebody you have never heard of. You can usually take it for granted that the author of the glowing testimonial to the man whose story you are about to read was also the writer of the book. Once in a while, *really* outstanding personalities of the ring will inherit two, three, or even more outside biographers. These can range from serious studies like Donald Barr Chidsey's excellent *Life and Times of John L. Sullivan* to the saccharine and cloying *Brown Bomber*, a Joe Louis opus by sob-sister Margery Miller.

Of course, prizefighters these days are a lot more articulate than they used to be. If they are not actually comfortable with the pen or the typewriter, the tape-recorder and television microphones hold no fears for them. There has probably never been a sporting figure quite so glib as Cassius Clay, for instance, who, contracting in December for a fight, say, three months ahead, could yet ask : 'How long till February?' The late Rocky Marciano, too, whose ring style suggested that he might be the original 'dese, dem an' dose' kid, was, in fact, surprisingly coherent and literate. Terry Downes, whose Anglo-American idiom, spoken with a cockney accent which is often barely intelligible, largely through a severely-chastised organ he refers to as his "ooter', is nevertheless one of the quickest-witted and amusing raconteurs to whom I have ever had the pleasure of listening. I am pretty sure that I know who wrote Downes's story of his left and career, *My Bleeding Business,* but I am also pretty sure that that competent and highly-professional gentleman had far less trouble with his material, probably taped, than many earlier ghosts.

* * *

I have suggested that almost every great fighter sooner or later produces a book of some sort, and/or a biography or two by other hands. I should like to mention a few of the more enjoyable books of this type that I have come across. I should also like to stress the fact that you will find very few of them these days on your public library shelves or those of the bookshops. Most have long since been out of print. But almost all of them are listed in the vast British Museum catalogue, so anyone with sufficient keenness could have a silent orgy of reading, once possessed of a ticket to the famous Reading Room. If you are enthusiastic enough to start a collection of books about boxing you will always find a second-hand bookseller somewhere in your district who will advertise for the titles you want through the trade's invaluable journal, *The Clique*. It is subscribed to by dealers all over the world, and every week there is a brisk exchange of reports and orders. I have both bought and sold many books through this medium. The prices you will eventually be quoted will depend upon the condition and the scarcity of the books in question.

Shortly before John L. Sullivan defended his world's title versus James J. Corbett in 1892, a Boston publisher produced *The Life and Reminiscences of a Nineteenth Century Gladiator*. It was brought out just at the time when it was thought that most interest was being shown in Sullivan, and certainly the excitement of the old Boston Strong Boy's return to the ring after so long sold a large number of copies. Still, it is a pity that the book is incomplete, in that it lacks the story of his last and most publicised fight.

However, this was remedied by Corbett himself, many years later – in 1925, to be precise – when he issued *The Roar of the Crowd* with the aid of Robert Gordon Anderson. It was originally published in New York, but it has since been re-issued in this country, and it shouldn't be difficult to find.

Corbett's conqueror, Bob Fitzsimmons, tells his own story in *Ruby Robert*. It is a good yarn, but it is expressed in such high-flown and 'literary' prose that although it gives us all the facts it is evident from page one that Fitzsimmons himself had little to do with it.

Jim Jeffries, too, probably had the minimum to do with

the production of *Two Fisted Jeff*, published in 1929. In fact, although this book is in the first peron, and is ostensibly by Jeffries, the by-line on the title-page is that of Hugh Fullerton.

Tommy Burns, who was next in line among the heavyweight champions, has no autobiography of which I am aware. He did, however, lend his name to a text-book on boxing, but it deals very little with the bouts of his own career.

Jack Johnson's 1927 opus, *In the Ring – and Out,* is probably the most interesting of all these books of reminiscences. It is a fascinating tale, but one not always accurate as regards the facts. You must take this one with a very large pinch of salt, although it has great value in revealing aspects of Johnson's unique personality. It carries so many introductory articles that it is hard to tell which of their authors, if any of them, was responsible for actually writing Johnson's book for him. Complementary with this work is Finis Farr's *Black Champion,* which came out in 1964. Sub-titled 'The Life and Times of Jack Johnson', it certainly tells as much of the times as the life. It is a revealing work, but the great coloured fighter's actual ring appearances are largely glossed over or disposed of summarily.

Johnson's conqueror, Jess Willard, had a pretty undistinguished career, apart from the fight which won him the title and the slaughter in which he lost it. This may be why nobody ever thought it worth approaching him about publishing his life story. At least, if it was ever done, the book has eluded me.

Jack Dempsey had several books written about him, of course. One of the first was executed by Nat Fleischer, editor of the monthly magazine, *The Ring.* It is entitled *Jack Dempsey – the Idol of Fistiana.* Try to get hold of the first edition, if you can, which came out in 1929. It is profusely illustrated with many photographs of Dempsey's early fights and opponents, and its main interest, for me, lies in these pictures. Unhappily, when Fleischer brought out a new and revised edition, in 1936, he added a little text and jettisoned many of these rarely-seen photos. Dempsey's own official story of his career, *Round by Round,* is a much better book, as far as the reading matter is concerned.

Gene Tunney, Dempsey's successor, was also 'done' by

Fleischer in an effort called *Gene Tunney – the Enigma of the Ring,* but here again the principal's own work, far more intimate and revealing, outshines the mere cataloguing and outside reporting of events by the journalist. Tunney didn't particularly like the idea of other people writing about him at length and with apparent authority, and he did nothing to endear himself to those of the scribbling profession with his remarks on four biographies of himself he had seen. 'They were so inaccurate from beginning to end that to me they were more amusing than historical.' I always thought that this rankled a little with Nat Fleischer: he probably suspected that *his* life of Tunney was one of those four. When a naïve correspondent, some years later, asked *The Ring*'s question and answer page which was the better book, Fleischer's or Tunney's, the reply was inevitable: Fleischer's. 'Gene thinks too much of Gene,' was the comment. Admittedly, this champion, like most others, was not particularly modest. But then, he hadn't much to be modest about.

Schmeling, Sharkey, Carnera, Baer and Braddock, those fighters who came after Tunney in the early and middle Thirties, all had their Boswells in Sunday newspaper serialisations, and one or two gained the distinction of seeing their stories in hard covers, but the finished products were not impressive. Nor, for that matter, were the flood of publications about Joe Louis, who followed them, and who humbled them all between June, 1935 and June, 1938.

The first was premature, to say the very least. It came out in 1935, after Louis had just won his first important fight, and had been a professional for less than a year! Others followed at intervals during his long and eventful career. The official autobiography, entitled *My Life Story,* which deals with fights and happenings up to 1947, and the Tami Mauriello contest, is by far the best.

Both Ezzard Charles and Jersey Joe Walcott, next in line of succession, have been written about, of course, but in my opinion very little of the production is worthwhile. Rocky Marciano, too, who followed them, has yet to be adequately captured in book form. The same may be said for Floyd Patterson, Ingemar Johansson and Sonny Liston. Johansson did inspire a highly-extravagant eulogy entitled *Varldsmastarnas*

Varldsmastare, by Tore Nilsson, in Stockholm in 1959, after he surprisingly knocked out Patterson in three rounds, but it looks pretty silly in the light of his two return contests and more recent events.

Inevitably, a figure so controversial as Cassius Clay has attracted more than one biographer, but the best thing about him that I have read, strangely enough, deals very little with his deeds within the ropes and is more of a psychological study than anything else, and was published too soon. Clay's own story, purportedly sold to a publisher for a considerable fortune, has yet to appear, at the time of writing. I anticipate many books about this remarkable personality in the years to come.

There are, of course, a host of books about some of the more interesting and flamboyant characters in the lighter divisions. Carpentier attracted his first biography, *From Pit-Boy to Champion Boxer,* by F. Hurdman-Lucas, when he was still a teenage phenomenon. He had never been a pit-boy and was only a relatively minor champion at the time. His first autobiography, *My Fighting Life,* came out in 1920, in the wake of his thrilling one-round victory over Joe Beckett. It thus lacks the descriptions of his peak and decline. It was in 1955, when he was an elderly man, that he gave us *Carpentier – by Himself,* the full story of his career.

James R. Fair, a Pittsburgh newspaperman, offered the world *Give Him to the Angels* in 1946, roughly twenty years after his subject, the fabulous Harry Greb, had died on an operating table. It is not a life-story, strictly speaking, but more of a collection of racy anecdotes about an amazing character whose wild and riotous public and private life had long before placed him in the realm of legend. It has no chronological sequence, but suffers little from that. If only half the stories in it are true, and I suspect that many are apocryphal, then Harry Greb was a remarkable personality, indeed. Make an effort to get hold of this one.

Other stories well worth reading are Jimmy Wilde's *Fighting Was My Business,* Freddie Mills's *Twenty Years,* and, of course, that confession of the former delinquent, Rocky Graziano, *Somebody Up There Likes Me.* When Hollywood bought it as a starring vehicle for Paul Newman it had all the ingredients necessary for a successful feature film, and needed the minimum of adaptation.

Departing from those books ostensibly written by boxers, and those monographs about them, some of the most interesting reminiscences and memoirs have been those of referees. Eugene Corri, who officiated at most of the major bouts held in England during the decade preceding the First World War and in the ten years after it, gave us four books. They are *Thirty Years a Boxing Referee,* (1915), and *Refereeing a Thousand Fights,* (1919), which is much the same thing brought up to date, *Gloves and the Man,* (1927), and his definitive memoirs, *Fifty Years in the Ring,* which came out in 1933. Joe Palmer's *Recollections of a Boxing Referee,* which deals with roughly the same period covered by Corri, describes all the important contests in which *he* officiated. A much later work is Moss De Yong's *Everybody Boo.* The title is an apt one. I saw this avuncular character in action many times, but I can recall no occasion when he climbed through the ropes without the accompaniment of a chorus of derisive yells and catcalls. He was a perfectly capable referee, but the greeting was traditional. I doubt if ten in a thousand of the booers knew why they were doing it.

Among promoters and managers, the most interesting books I have read are William A. Brady's *The Fighting Man,* (1916), his *Showman,* (1937), and the several volumes of memoirs produced by Charles B. Cochran. While primarily a man of the theatre, Cochran took more than one fling at the ring, in the spheres of both boxing and wrestling, during his long and eventful career. One of his hobbies would appear to have been producing books of reminiscences. He published *Secrets of a Showman* in 1925, *Cock-a-Doodle-Do* in 1941, and *A Showman Looks On* in 1945. Each of these volumes has some interesting sections on his flirtation with boxing promotion.

Mrs Tex Rickard lent her name to *Everything Happened to Him,* a book about her incredible money-making husband: the man who was responsible for the million-dollar gate in pugilism. I find this one valuable for the information it imparts, but almost impossible to read with any pleasure because of its cloying, sentimental and *Peg's Paper* type of style.

I have always thought it a pity that more of the famous

boxing managers of the first half of the century did not some-how get their stories down on to paper. Yet, on reflection, I suppose it is not surprising. The methods of many of them were devious, to put it mildly, and some were out and out crooks in their efforts to get the best deal they could. James J. Johnston, for instance, was an engaging rogue known far and wide as 'The Boy Bandit', for very good reason. Marcus Griffin told Johnston's story in *Wise Guy,* or as much of it as he knew. I fancy that a few of his contemporaries like Joe Jacobs, Jack Kearns and Al Weill could have added a lot more. Among the autobiographies of British managers, Ted Broadribb's *Fighting is my Life* and Charlie Rose's *Life's a Knockout* are well worth reading. I suppose that between them, this pair guided the affairs and destinies of more native-born top-notchers than any dozen other managers. They have some good yarns to tell.

Many efforts have been made at a complete history of boxing. The subject, of course, is a vast one. Covering the London Prize Ring alone, Pierce Egan's *Boxiana* was the earliest. It runs to five volumes, which were published between 1812 and 1825, and therefore lacks even mention of heroes like Bendigo, Tom Sayers and John C. Heenan. Henry Downes Miles, who wrote the enormous *Pugilistica,* and which extends to over five hundred pages in each of the three large octavo volumes of the 1906 edition, never thought a lot of Egan as a historian, and refers to him as 'illiterate'. Downes's work is much more complete and reliable, and deals with every bare-knuckle fight and fighter of importance. Egan is the racier of the two, but it is suspected that many of his descriptive battles were born of his vivid imagination.

It was not until 1927 that both the Prize Ring and the Queensberry Ring were adequately dealt with in one volume, and then it only covered boxing in America, by Alexander Johnston in his *Ten – and Out!* Later editions brought it up to date, but it necessarily glosses over much on which one feels the author could have been greatly entertaining if he had had the space. I think Johnston is far more readable than Nat Fleischer, who gave us his *The Heavyweight Championship* in

1949. Fleischer knew his stuff – none better – when telling us what happened in the many fights he dealt with, but he was a prolific and overworked journalist at all times. I find him an excellent cataloguer and researcher but a somewhat slap-dash writer. He produced a formidable number of books about boxing and boxers over something like fifty years. I think his major contributions are the editing of his monthly magazine, *The Ring,* for roughly the same period, and the enormous *Pictorial History of Boxing,* which he produced in collaboration with Sam André.

There are many books about the ring which do not attempt to paint the whole picture, and which make enjoyable reading. Most of these were written by sporting journalists and reporters : men who, in most instances, had known the fighters they were writing about. Of those books emanating from this country, I would strongly recommend the following : Harry Furniss's *By Ways and Queer Ways of Boxing,* profusely illustrated by the author, who was also an accomplished black and white artist, cartoonist and caricaturist; James Butler's *Kings of the Ring*; Ben Bennison's *Champions on Parade*; Fred Dartnell's *Seconds Out!,* and the many books by Trevor Wignall, which include *The Story of Boxing* (1923), *The Sweet Science* (1926), *Prides of the Fancy* (1928) and *Ringside* (1941). He wrote several others, which extend to various sports and the occasions he covered for his newspapers, and he also, as he said, 'took a whirl at fiction'. Unhappily, this medium was not his forte : I doubt if you will ever find the name of Trevor Wignall in any history of English literature. Among the American productions that have impressed me are *Champions Off Guard,* by William O. Inglis, and what is, to me, the most entertaining book ever written on the sport, by A. J. Liebling. Its author chose to call it *The Sweet Science,* either not knowing, or possibly not caring, that Wignall had used it some thirty years previously. There is no copyright on titles. Liebling chose a limited time-range : his writing in this book is confined to that era dominated by Rocky Marciano, and he deals fascinatingly with that champion's fights versus Jersey Joe Walcott and Archie Moore. He also touches upon the careers of the young Floyd Patterson, Ray Robinson and Randolph Turpin, as well as that of the amazing featherweight, Sandy Saddler. I have enjoyed everything that Liebling wrote and that I have read, whether it were straight newspaper reporting, essays in *The New Yorker,* or his gastronomic symphonies in prose form. My one regret is that he did not do more of what his editor once called his 'low-life pieces'. His ring essays, celebrating near-Runyon characters like Whitey Bimstein, Charley Goldman and Al Weill would come under this heading.

I have encountered much fiction dealing with boxing, but very little of it has the ring of authenticity, as it were. Certain highlights usually find their way into anthologies, and are frequently quoted as examples of masterpieces. One is 'The Smith's Last Battle', a chapter from Arthur Conan Doyle's *Rodney Stone.* Another is the same author's short story, *The Croxley Master,* but I must admit that this did not impress me much when I read it. Jack London's two novels, *The Game* and *The Abysmal Brute,* have also been lauded, but both disappointed me. Admittedly, I was prejudiced in favour of the sport, and London was taking a knock at it, but I was disappointed for a different reason, too. I have seen too many fights in real life to be able to believe in fictional ones where the hero is a superman, so good in every department of the sport that he can name the round, the minute, and even the very second of terminating a bout.

Bernard Shaw, in a very long and active life, was 'ag'in' many things: capitalism, meat-eating, drinking, smoking, vivisection and vaccination are a few which come readily to mind. Not altogether surprisingly, he was 'ag'in' prize-fighting, too. Here, I mean prize-fighting in its strictest sense: fighting for money. But this did not deter him from admiring the art of boxing, or from appreciating the talents of two of its better practitioners, Carpentier and Tunney. While he felt it incumbent upon him to wage war against professional pugilism, he nevertheless loved a good scrap all his life. I suspect that he 'could use 'em a bit' himself in his younger days, although it is difficult to conjure the image of the spindly, bearded sage with the gloves on. He certainly knew what he was talking about when he held forth upon the art of boxing. As a young man of twenty-six he wrote a novel centred on the ring, called *Cashel Byron's Profession*. In his later years, a highly-successful dramatist and pamphleteer, he offered it to the public as one of the 'novels of my nonage'. I do not recommend it as a good boxing story, but I strongly urge that you seek out the 'right' edition, which carries both his later-written preface at the beginning and his tongue-in-cheek Elizabethan blank-verse dramatisation of the novel, *The Admirable Bashville,* at the end. In the first you will find some of the best sense ever written about boxing and prize-fighting, as an art, and in the second you will get the gist of the long-winded Victorian novel, *Cashel Byron's Profession,* which lies between the two.

The best novel I have ever read about the ring is Budd Schulberg's *The Harder They Fall*. It is based on the career of that unfortunate freak, Primo Carnera, and while it eulogises the sport no more than Jack London's books, it is wonderful stuff. You can almost smell the sweat and liniment of the sleazy gyms, you come to know Jacobs's Beach for what it really was, and there is no attempt to romanticise. On the other hand, Jim Tully's *The Bruiser,* while highly authentic, reeks of romanticism as well. Tully was a former illiterate Irish-American hobo and itinerant pug, who suddenly sat down one day and started to write. His first novel, *Emmett Lawler,* largely autobiographical and also dealing with the professional ring, was originally submitted to a publisher in one whole paragraph! Editors put that right, of course, but as the years progressed, Jim Tully's forthright style changed considerably. Nearly twenty years later, in *The Bruiser,* he was inclined to keep his paragraphs down to one short, florid, but highly descriptive sentence. His account of the great championship fight, the climax of the book, is one of the most exciting I have ever read.

If Ernest Hemingway had never made a reputation for himself as the first coherent Anglo-Saxon apologist for the bull-fight, he would surely be largely remembered for his pre-occupation with boxing. Allusions to, and analogies with the ring abound throughout his published works. And if *The Undefeated* is the best short story ever written celebrating *los toros,* then surely *Fifty Grand* is the finest boxing tale in the same medium. It is loosely based on that famous bout in 1922, when Benny Leonard fouled himself out of the fight versus Jack Britton to save his reputation. Hemingway improved on that ending, demonstrating that if truth is stranger than fiction, then fiction can be infinitely more entertaining than truth. In the story, Jack Brennan (Britton), approaching the end of his career, believes that he cannot beat his challenger, Walcott (Leonard), and secretly bets $50,000 on his more youthful and stronger opponent. After outboxing the younger man for the earlier part of the fight, Brennan fades, and begins to take the beating he felt was inevitable. The climax comes in the thirteenth round, when Walcott deliberately sinks a punch well below the belt. Brennan keeps his feet, knowing that if he goes down the referee will assuredly declare him the winner and the money will be lost. With great courage he stays erect and fouls Walcott in return, and is immediately disqualified. It may not be particularly edifying, but it is great writing. 'It's funny how fast you can think when it means that much money,' says Brennan.

I have always regretted that Hemingway never had the time or inclination to give us a big book about boxing something like his famous classic of the bulls, *Death in the Afternoon*. He certainly knew far more about the subject than all but the best of the professional commentators, as he proved in many of his shorter pieces.

Buy, beg, borrow or steal a novel by A. G. Hales called *Nut-Brown Maid and Nut-Brown Mare*, if ever you come across it. I say that because it's years since I handled a copy, and I know for a fact that it's hard to come by. If you are keen enough to advertise or search for it, don't be misled or fobbed off by another book with a similar title, by Philip Lindsay. If you are, you will be disappointed. Of the two, Lindsay's book is undoubtedly the better literature, but it's not what you will be looking for. The book I'm talking about now is literature only in the broadest sense of the term. It is a glorious Piece of Hokum, sired by Utter Tripe out of Pure Corn – but then A. G. Hales never had any pretensions to being another Shakespeare.

He was a tough and grizzled Aussie, hard-living and hard-drinking, who got into journalism more or less accidentally, by way of general knocking about and adventuring. He embodied all the old popular virtues, like patriotism, chivalry, and one hundred per cent masculinity. He was what used to be called 'a man's man'. He would have been proud to have been called one, but if you had read a *double entendre* into the term he'd have socked you in the jaw. He worshipped fighters, athletes, soldiers, sailors and – beautiful women. When he started writing books he took as his subjects fighters, athletes, soldiers, sailors and, of course, beautiful women. He was literate, but hardly literary. He would possibly have accepted poets as being necessary, but would have lauded Rudyard Kipling and Robert W. Service rather than Percy Bysshe Shelley or W. H. Auden. He would have plumped for Jack London's prose and subject matter but would have abhorred those of Ronald Firbank.

For the most part, he wrote rollicking adventure stories around a dare-devil, swashbuckling and ugly character whom he called McGluskey. The books sold in their many thousands, and were read by millions. Forty years ago the public and circulating libraries were full of them. They were literally read to pieces. I discovered him myself in the early nineteen-thirties, when Jack Doyle, at that time in the dog-house with the British Boxing Board of Control, elected to earn his bread as an actor in a film based on Hales's *McGluskey the Sea Rover*: a triumph of miscasting if ever there was one.

As a not particularly discriminating literary critic in my teens, even I could evaluate A. G. Hales. He wrote a florid, rambling and discursive prose with characters and plots that were outrageously larger than life. I was never sufficiently enamoured of his books to read them all, but a couple did impress me. Hales had an extraordinary facility for weaving fact and fiction into his narratives, a sort of documentary approach which, as far as I know, had never been done before. Thus, I recall that the opening scene of *Nut-Brown Maid* is set in the vast bowl at Reno, on 4 July, 1910, when Jim Jeffries came out of retirement to do battle with the coloured 'upstart', Jack Johnson. Throughout the book real people mingle with his imaginary characters. Again, I recall that in one of the McGluskey books Georges Carpentier turns up for a brief 'guest appearance', so to speak, and in another McGluskey episode, dealing with seal-poaching, if I remember correctly, one of the youthful bar-room drinkers is a good-looking and broad-shouldered tough guy called Jack London. This famous writer *did,* in fact, frequent those saloons in his young days, and for a brief period was an oyster pirate. These touches added a certain verisimilitude to A. G. Hales's yarns.

He surpassed himself in this direction with a fictionalised biography of the great Australian Negro pugilist, Peter Jackson, called *Black Prince Peter.* Irving Stone did the same sort of thing years later, of course, with books like *Lust for Life* (Van Gogh), and *The Agony and the Ecstasy* (Michelangelo), just as Shakespeare had done hundreds of years earlier with some of his dramatic histories. When I first read *Black Prince Peter,* I was young and naïve enough to look upon it as straight biography, and could not understand why librarians insisted upon putting the book on their fiction shelves. Hollywood did this sort of thing wonderfully, taking world-famous characters like Florenz Ziegfeld, Al Jolson, Eddie Duchin and Cole Porter, and telling their 'stories' in lavish musicals which were great entertainment but utterly phoney. Jolson, for one, is well known to have been a sinner : *The Jolson Story* makes him out to have been almost a saint. A. G. Hales did much the same thing with Peter Jackson. There is a tradition in boxing that this particular practitioner was a fine and honourable man, and I have no reason to doubt it. Seventy years ago he was termed 'the whitest black man who ever lived'. This was considered quite a compliment by many at the time : rather less so at the present day. What Jackson thought about it we are not told. He was certainly liked and respected by the gentry at the National Sporting Club, probably because, unlike Jack Johnson, he was 'a nigger who knew his place'. Yet I find it difficult to believe that Jackson did not have his fair share of human foibles and weaknesses. However, be that as it may, Hales sat down and wrote 'the life' of this pugilist in a curious blend of fact and fiction in which his hero is really too goody-goody to be true. The descriptions of the fights, those versus Slavin, Corbett, Jeffries, etc., are authentic enough, and are very well done. The account of Jackson's life outside the ring, of which the author could have known few of the actual details, shouldn't

188

really have been done at all. Hales poured on the schmaltz with a ladle.

With regard to the humorous side of boxing, I can think of no writer on our side of the Atlantic who has written anything really funny about the sport, in the way, say, that A. G. Macdonell wrote about cricket, and there are precious few from the United States. H. C. Witwer attempted to do so in the nineteen-twenties, and he had a considerable success with a number of books on the lighter side of boxing and baseball. They date terribly these days and, for the most part written in the New York vernacular, they never had much of an appeal in Britain at the time. Witwer was, perhaps, a minor Ring Lardner: derivative certainly, and to some extent imitative. If any British middle-aged readers recall him at all, it will be through *The Leather Pushers,* which was made into a successful Hollywood serial film, and which also had some success over here. Witwer was very fond of punning, and wrote books with titles like *A Smile a Minute, There's No Base Like Home,* and *Love and Learn.* In 1927 he produced *The Classics in Slang,* narrated by 'One Punch' McTague, a 'twenty-eight-carat bum' who relates the basic plots of works by Shakespeare, Dumas, Hugo, Dickens, *et al,* with frequent references and analogies to his robust profession. *Yes Man's Land,* published a couple of years later, tells what happens when a pleasure-loving young boxer succumbs to the blandishments of Hollywood.

The aforementioned Ring Lardner, a short-story writer rather than a novelist, wrote many amusing tales with sporting backgrounds. His *Alibi Ike,* about baseball, is one of his better-known. *A Frame-Up* is probably the funniest story he ever wrote about the ring. It can be found in the collection called *Round Up, the Stories of Ring W. Lardner,* (1935).

His contemporary, Damon Runyon, has enjoyed far more popularity in Britain, although his short stories, for which he is most famous, concentrate upon the gangsters, gamblers and low-lifers along that short strip of Broadway between Times Square and Columbus Circle. Most of his boxing reporting, confined to newspapers, is hardly known at all in Britain.

In 1934, Runyon contributed a foreword to a very funny book by a fellow-newspaperman, Don Skene. It is called *The Red Tiger*. Runyon began : 'This story is one of the grandest pieces of humor and satire that I have ever read.' I agree entirely. The book tells of how Merle Gillingwater, a timid but enormous young red-head, is built up as James J. Clancy, the Red Tiger of the Rockies, to become heavyweight champion of the world, defeating Wing J. Wong, the Wild Dragon of the Yangtze. Doc Carey, his manager, bears more than a close resemblance to the real-life Jack Kearns and James J. Johnston, both in his methods and in the many black and white illustrations dotted throughout the book. I have read many works with extravagant eulogies in the blurb like 'a punch on every page', or 'a laugh in every line'. *The Red Tiger* is the only book I have ever encountered where one might say, quite literally, that there is a wisecrack in almost every sentence.

Paul Gallico is known throughout Europe as the best-selling author of such tender tales as *The Snow Goose* and *The Lonely,* and his extremely humorous books in a much lighter vein. I first encountered him nearly forty years ago when he was the hard-bitten sports columnist of the New York *Daily News* and innovator of the now famous Golden Gloves amateur boxing tournament, which produced Joe Louis, among others. He once wrote an amusing short story called *The Roman Kid,* which strangely enough, eventually found its place in an anthology as a classic example of the detective tale ! It tells of how an American sports reporter, Gallico himself, as it happens, goes to the Museo delle Terme in Rome, sees the life-size bronze statue of the Roman gladiator known as the Sitting Boxer, and makes some interesting deductions. The statue has only recently been excavated, and not much is known about it, or even if it is genuine. The brash reporter, in the faces of the dry-as-dust, learned antiquarians and archaeologists who doubt its authenticity, proceeds to do a real Sherlock Holmes job on the bronze by virtue of his wide knowledge and acquaintance of the ring, proving, among other things, that the gladiator had been a southpaw. It is a remarkable little tale, and may be found in Gallico's *Confessions of a Story-Teller,* first published in this country in 1961, together with his story behind this story.

There is one final book I must mention: it does not quite fit into any of the categories above.

In 1921, at a time when Georges Carpentier looked to be a certainty, on this side of the ocean, to beat Jack Dempsey for the heavyweight championship of the world, a work of fiction – no less – was published under his name! Who actually wrote it I do not know, and I have no knowledge of how much, if anything, Carpentier contributed towards it. The book makes no pretensions in the direction of great literature: it is a crime-thriller with a boxing background. Further, from its 'bumper book' appearance: coloured cloth boards, large and easily-read, thick and heavy paper of the 'pulp' variety to make the volume bulky, and its numerous black and white full-page illustrations, it would appear that *Brothers of the Brown Owl* was aimed at the juvenile market. Its complete lack of any feminine romantic interest also tends to suggest this. Indeed, I first came across it in the school library at the age of about nine or ten, among books like Max Pemberton's *The Black Pirate* and Fenimore Cooper's *Last of the Mohicans.* It is a fair yarn, with the hero, a handsome and debonair French pugilist, bearing remarkable similarities to the man whose name appears on the title-page. I was struck, at the time, by the illustrations by George Bates. The hero, in action within the ropes, looked *very* much like Carpentier. And for good reason! Some years later, when I came across Carpentier's 1914 text-book, *My Methods,* the posed photographic illustrations appeared unusually familiar. You will find that almost every one of the fight drawings in *Brothers of the Brown Owl* is a black and white copy of one of the photos in the earlier opus.

I have, of course, only skimmed across the surface of this subject here. I am aware of two published bibliographies on boxing. One, by Paul Magriel, lists the books written about it, but unfortunately stops short at that period when bare fists went out and padded gloves came in. The second is *The History and Bibliography of Boxing Books* by Robert Hartley, which is a most important full-scale reference work.

26 Old-Timers Versus Moderns

I think it is in one of Somerset Maugham's plays that a character defines that time of life when middle-age has imperceptibly crept up on one. 'Have you noticed how all the policemen seem so much younger than they used to be?' Similarly, I suppose the follower of boxing, or of any entertainment or endeavour for that matter, may be said to be no longer young when he begins to compare the current crop of fighters, film stars, crooners and courtesans with those of his enthusiastic youth. Invariably the old days and the old 'uns were better. This holds good for both the amateur and the professional observer.

Years ago, in common with many another young exuberant, I could never understand why my contemporaries in the ring should always be knocked at the expense of those my father had seen, and I would use the old argument that had been used countless times before. Runners were undoubtedly faster than they had been, and were going to get faster still, jumpers were jumping higher and longer all the time, and weight-lifters continued to clip the records. Why, I asked, shouldn't present-day boxers be better than the old-timers? While the earlier historians of pugilism had made gods of the Sullivans and Corbetts of the eighteen-eighties and eighteen-nineties, and one could not deny them their stamina and courage, it was difficult for the brash adolescent to get over those corny photographs and the stilted stances they portrayed. A Dempsey of the nineteen-twenties would surely have knocked them cold before they could get those fists up into their elegant poses? Today, of course, Jack Dempsey looks equally corny in his voluminous knee-length shorts and cropped haircut.

But my faith in the prowess of my contempories first took a real jolt when I was given the unique opportunity of watching the film of a contest between two men whose names were not mentioned on the titles at the start simply because there weren't any titles. The owner of the film did not know who the men were either, and he wanted me to try and identify them. A previous owner of the film, with misguided helpfulness, had scrawled on the leader, in ink, the inscription: 'Moir and Jackson', which made no sense. When the film started, I saw immediately that the men were either featherweights or light-weights, and I guessed the time of the fight as being twentieth century but definitely pre-war. The Kaiser's war, that is, not the Fuhrer's. The fight was probably round about the time of the Johnson-Jeffries contest. I deduced this not only from the fact that it was held in sunlight and from the style of clothes the seconds, the referee and a few of the spectators were wearing, but from the very little the boxers themselves had on. One wore loose-fitting trunks with a knotted sash and the other had a pair of shorts so abbreviated as to be little more than a jock-strap: ring apparel which would not be allowed in more recent and more regulated days.

The fight itself was something to remember. One man was a fighter who never stopped attacking for a second, and the other was a boxer whose artistry was so superb that his aggressive opponent never succeeded in landing a really solid and damaging punch. Not that the boxer was wholly defensive: he met his man with some pretty vicious digs and swipes himself, although at first these did not seem to make much impression. The fighter was a glutton for the boxer's punches and refused to take a backward step. I had never seen a pugilist take so much so forcibly and still keep coming.

The boxer appeared to be able to change his style and tactics at will: a versatility I had never seen in the hundreds of flesh-and-blood contests I had watched. He was a combination of scientific defender, precise and accurate attacker, and ruthless puncher. I was enthralled, although I did not blind myself to the knowledge that against a man of his opponent's type he was made to appear twice as good as he really was.

This battle went on for eleven rounds before the boxer's more educated talents overcame the fighter's spirited but more downright and mundane gifts. It ended after several knock-downs, culminating in a thrilling knock-out. I never hope to see a more interesting and inspiring contest.

From his looks, I hesitantly identified the boxer as Owen Moran. Yet I doubted my own opinion, since I had not thought Moran was anywhere as good as that. The fighter was harder still. He looked like Battling Nelson from his style and garb, but he was never still long enough for me to get a good look at his face. I did not have a record book by me to check, but the scrawled 'Moir and Jackson' now appeared to be a good rough guess by someone who had once been told the right names of the men and had later forgotten them.

My friend, G. Neville Weston, whose investigations into the byways and backwaters of both cricketing and boxing history would have elicited the admiration of Sherlock Holmes, one of his idols, saw this film himself shortly afterwards. He confirmed that it was indeed the meeting between Moran and Nelson, which ended in the eleventh round and was the first time the Battler was knocked out in his life.

Although I was proud to have my identification corroborated by such an authority, my conclusions had to undergo some drastic revisions after seeing that film. I had read a lot about the old-time lightweights and how tough they were and how much better they had fought than our modern men. I had taken all this in without really thinking much about it. Now I knew it was true, and perhaps the difference was greater than even the boosters had believed.

Blind patriotism and partisanship has never been one of my virtues, but I felt rather proud of Owen Moran for having been a Britisher. If Britain could produce boxers like that then we could excuse the old country for a few of the others. But why did the American critics always remember the stinkers and seldom mention men like Moran?

This pugilist flourished at a time when the ranks were full of first-class featherweights and lightweights. Abe Attell, Ad Wolgast, Frankie Neil, Packy McFarland, Jim Driscoll and Matt Wells were a few of the men he fought. Jimmy Britt,

Willie Ritchie, Freddie Welsh and Leach Cross were his contemporaries. If men of this calibre could live in the same ring with him, and some of them even *beat* him, what price some of our present-day pugs, catapulted into the big time after perhaps a dozen fights against men with no more experience than themselves?

As I say, I revised my opinions, and viewed the oldsters with a new respect. But I was still able to watch a contest between youngsters without sneering. However, as time went by I found it more and more difficult to work up enthusiasm over the newest and latest phenomena the ring offered. In the heavy-weight class alone, a division which has always commanded the larger part of my interest, the more recent practitioners appeared to me to lack talent, colour or personality. I would look at the list of title contenders among the big men and ask myself how many of their names would mean anything at all to the man in the street. Then I would think back to the early Thirties, for example, when I was a young man, and remember the heavyweights who were fighting among themselves for precedence and a chance at the championship. They boxed not once or twice a year, but sometimes every month. They seemed to count for something then, and Mr Average Man had at least heard of them.

Inevitably, my enthusiasm waned, but I still kept track of current pugilistic events, and wrote about them, too. But more and more I found myself inclined to wax reminiscent and nostalgic when holding forth for the delectation of my juniors. But I always felt a little uneasy. *Are* the policeman of today younger than those of my youth?

Then I remember Joe Louis, and I am comforted. I consider myself fortunate in that I was about when this man was meeting and beating any fighter who had the temerity to climb into a ring with him. For several years during his career his talents were so far beyond those of his fellow-practitioners that he really looked like a superman. It seemed that he would go on for ever and could never be beaten. He became a living legend. He was so long at the top that in the end he was fighting men who had been of schoolboy age when he had won the title. Even the most fervid boosters of the ancients had to admit that Louis compared favourably with their heroes. A few admitted that Joe could have licked them all. It was inevitable, perhaps, that the sport should have entered the doldrums for a time when the healthy trade winds of Joe Louis blew out.

But was it inevitable that many of the men afterwards – some of them Negroes inspired directly by his career – should prove to be so colourless? Even Marciano, who staged some pretty good fights during his reign, and who came to be viewed as one of the best, in retrospect, could not arouse the excitement and attract the gates that Louis had done even when every city for miles around the arena was 'blacked out' as far as televising his fights was concerned. And always remember that there has been far more money in the fight fans' pockets since the Second World War than there was in the years just before it. Remember, too, that back in those Dark Ages, after Dempsey and Tunney had retired and the United States was in the middle of an economic depression, the unpopular Jack Sharkey was responsible for some amazingly high box-office receipts, considering the times. Perhaps the public did turn out hoping to see him beaten, but at least they did turn out.

Of course, I can never insist whole-heartedly that the standard of boxing is continually lowering and that I have remained unaltered and immaculate in my approach to the ring. I am ready to concede that much of the fault lies within me : the ardent zeals of youth are gone and I have grown blasé and cynical. This is strongly impressed upon me when I hear young men of my acquaintance enthusing about current boxers who only bore me, and who rush to buy tickets with both fervour and hard-earned money in order to see contests I just want to run away from. This leads me to recall my own juvenile and teenage predilections. Were those boxers of thirty and forty years ago very little different, after all, from those now in the public eye?

Many of them were no better and no worse, of course, but with the best will in the world I cannot deny some of them a glamour that rarely exists these days. I say rarely, and for very good reason. Cassius Clay compares favourably, in almost every respect, with any of the great old-timers, and this ranges from his ability within the ropes to his headline-making activities outside them. During his enforced sojourn in the wilderness during the late Sixties he said many times: 'I don't need boxing, but boxing needs me.' He never uttered a truer sentence in his life.

27   Apocryphal – IV

No boxer who ever lived had so much utter rot written about him as that remarkable little man, Jimmy Wilde. He boxed as a flyweight, and the maximum for this, the lightest of all divisions in the professional ring, is 112 lb., which is exactly eight stone. For a considerable part of his undoubtedly phenomenal career Wilde weighed much less than this limit. He did so well that on occasion he was obliged to box men who were a lot heavier than he was. I concede that Wilde often beat bantamweights (eight stone six pounds), even featherweights (nine stone), and maybe lightweights (nine stone nine) – although it would be difficult to find any listed in his record. But I doubt very much that the admittedly remarkable Jimmy Wilde was really the Paul Bunyan of the boxing ring that so many writers have made him out to be.

At one extreme I have read of his normal boxing weight as being six stone ten, with Wilde weighing in, fully-clothed and wearing an overcoat, *still* under the eight stone limit. At the other extreme, I have read of him boxing a light-heavyweight, in the gym, and putting that particular light-heavyweight temporarily out of action.

As I say, these are extremes. I am prepared to grant you that at some stage in his career Wilde boxed at six stone ten, and maybe he was wily enough to step on to the scales on one or two occasions wearing an overcoat in order to conceal his true poundage before he boxed a heavier man. He *may*, even, have clouted Boy McCormick, the light-heavyweight in question, with a punch which made that worthy stumble. But the legend has now grown to the extent that Jimmy Wilde, a tiny tot with pipe-stem arms and legs, so frail and sickly-looking that the promoters of his fights stood praying that he would not be killed, willingly took on men of all weights and sizes and knocked out boxers of any weight from fly to heavy!

It is a good story, but it is rot. Most photographs of Jimmy Wilde, in action, will show him as being a quite well-covered little man not particularly dwarfed by the one he is opposing. Those photographs offered of Wilde, the Mighty Midget, are posed pictures taken of him at the start of his career, when he *was* undersized and apparently puny. He had a magnificent career, but the fact remains that on the one occasion when he stepped out of his class and met a heavier man who was also a first-rater he took a bad beating.

The legend developed during his fighting life and in the nineteen-twenties, after he had retired. Wilde himself did nothing to discourage it: quite the reverse. Those who remember him, and met him, will recall that he was never backward in coming forward and blowing his own trumpet. When he died a few years ago some of the obituaries were ridiculous. The late George Whiting's story, in the London *Evening Standard,* made me wonder at the time if that highly-readable writer had ever seen Jimmy Wilde or only read the legend and swallowed it whole. His piece led me to write a letter to the editor, which was published a few days later. What a torrent of abuse descended upon my unsuspecting head! I learned very quickly that it was quite forbidden to twist the tail of *this* particular sacred cow, Jimmy Wilde. My brief education ranged from a retaliatory letter in the *Evening Standard* from an outraged reader who took the legend a few ridiculous steps further to abusive telephone calls from cranks at the crack of dawn. But not one of Jimmy Wilde's irate defenders could quote irrefutable chapter and verse.

If he could beat men who were 'twice his size', who were they? These would be men about as big, say, as Henry Cooper. If his punch was so formidable that he was able to knock men of this proportion kicking, even *after* he had retired, how come that he didn't literally kill every flyweight, bantamweight, featherweight and lightweight with the temerity to oppose him in his heyday?

Jimmy Wilde was the greatest flyweight boxer of all time, a little man with a natural but uncanny sense of timing which reinforced his punches as they caught opponents coming in and on to them. There is an 'alibi' for each one of his few defeats: the legend grew to such an extent that neither he nor his admirers would ever admit that he was beaten in fair fight. I believe that, in the long run, this will do a disservice to his memory.

An amusing footnote, discovered as I check my facts: my copy of the *All-Time Ring Record Book* gives Jimmy Wilde's weight as 108 lb., and his height as $2\frac{1}{2}$ inches. A Mighty Midget indeed.

Index